THE
BERLIN
SCHOOL

THE BERLIN SCHOOL

FILMS FROM THE BERLINER SCHULE

RAJENDRA ROY / ANKE LEWEKE

With contributions by Thomas Arslan, Valeska Grisebach,
Benjamin Heisenberg, Christoph Hochhäusler, Nina Hoss, Dennis Lim,
Katja Nicodemus, Christian Petzold, and Rainer Rother

The Museum of Modern Art, New York

Published in conjunction with the film series
The Berlin School: Films from the Berliner Schule
(November 20–December 6, 2013),
organized by Rajendra Roy and Anke Leweke

Produced by the Department of Publications,
The Museum of Modern Art, New York
Edited by Nancy Grubb
Designed by Pascale Willi
Production by Matthew Pimm

Translations from the German (all except texts by Rajendra Roy and Dennis Lim)
by Russell Stockman

Printed and bound by CS Graphics Sdn Bhd, Melaka, Malaysia .
This book was typeset in Apex. The paper is 150 gsm Furioso Matt.

Published by The Museum of Modern Art
11 West 53 Street
New York, New York 10019
www.moma.org

Distributed in the United States and Canada by ARTBOOK | D.A.P.
155 Sixth Avenue, 2nd floor, New York, New York 10013
www.artbook.com

Distributed outside the United States and Canada by
Thames & Hudson Ltd
181 High Holborn, London WC1V 7QX
www.thamesandhudson.com

Library of Congress Control Number: 2013941521
ISBN: 978-0-87070-874-9

Cover: Maren Ade. *Alle Anderen* (*Everyone Else*). 2009.
35mm film, color, 119 minutes. Lars Eidinger

Endpapers: Christian Petzold. *Gespenster* (*Ghosts*). 2005.
35mm film, color, 85 minutes. Sabine Timoteo and Julia Hummer (right)

Pages 4–5: Christian Petzold. *Jerichow*. 2008.
35mm film, color, 93 minutes. Benno Fürmann and Nina Hoss

Pages 18–19: Christoph Hochhäusler. *Unter dir die Stadt* (*The City Below*). 2010.
35mm film, color, 105 minutes. Robert Hunger-Bühler

Pages 30–31: Christian Petzold. *Barbara*. 2012. 35mm film, color, 105 minutes

Pages 44–45: Ulrich Köhler. *Montag kommen die Fenster* (*Windows on Monday*). 2006.
35mm film, color, 88 minutes. Isabelle Menke

Pages 58–59: Christian Petzold. *Barbara*. 2012.
Detail of production still. Nina Hoss

Pages 66–71: Valeska Grisebach. *Sehnsucht* (*Longing*). 2006.
16mm film blown up to 35mm, color, 88 minutes. Andreas Müller

Pages 72–73: Thomas Arslan. *Gold*. 2013. Digital video, color, 101 minutes

Pages 82–85: Thomas Arslan. *Geschwister* (*Brothers and Sisters*). 1997.
35mm film, color, 82 minutes. Production still. Left to right: Bülent Akil, Thomas Arslan,
Irina Hoppe, Bilge Bingül, and Tamer Yiğit

Pages 86–87: Maren Ade. *Alle Anderen* (*Everyone Else*). 2009.
Birgit Minichmayr and Lars Eidinger

Pages 98–101: Dressed-up hydrant seen in Vienna during location scouting for
Benjamin Heisenberg's *Der Räuber* (*The Robber*). 2008

Printed in Malaysia

Foreword

The Museum of Modern Art has long celebrated the impact of German filmmakers on global cinema. Ever since the late 1930s, when the Museum's first film curator, Iris Barry, traveled to Europe and began collecting film and ephemera from Germany, the Department of Film has dedicated significant time and resources to researching, collecting, preserving, and exhibiting this work. Our strong partnerships with such national institutions as the Deutsche Kinematek-Museum für Film und Fernsehen, the Bundesarchiv-Filmarchiv, and German Films, as well as many private foundations, have fostered a consequential series of exhibitions and publications over the decades. From *Weimar Cinema, 1919–1933: Daydreams and Nightmares* to *Rainer Werner Fassbinder* and *Werner Schroeter*, MoMA has presented a rich portrait of the movements and artists that make up Germany's cinematic history.

The Berlin School: Films from the Berliner Schule adds a new chapter to this narrative. A distinctly post-Wall phenomenon—originally just a loose affiliation of filmmakers working and studying in Berlin —it has no manifesto and rejects dogmatic practice. Nonetheless, the films of the Berlin School have resonated profoundly since the mid-1990s and now constitute one of the most influential auteur movements to emerge from Europe in the new millennium. The early Berlin School filmmakers Thomas Arslan, Christian Petzold, and Angela Schanelec are pivotal figures in German film history. The subsequent generations of Berlin School filmmakers have proven to be particularly adept at enunciating their vision in the cinephile community, fostering what the French critics have embraced as the "Nouvelle Vague Allemande" (German New Wave). Many of these filmmakers have contributed to this publication and will participate in the exhibition, and I thank them first and foremost.

This effort was led by Rajendra Roy, The Celeste Bartos Chief Curator of Film, and his co-curator and coauthor Anke Leweke. I applaud their many years of collaboration. I would also like to thank Christoph Hochhäusler, Dennis Lim, Katja Nicodemus, and Dr. Rainer Rother for their expert contributions to the publication, as well as Sophie Cavoulacos, Curatorial Assistant in the Department of Film, for her tireless shepherding of the project. Sincere thanks to Dieter Kosslick and his team at the Berlin International Film Festival for their nurturing of the Berlin School films and their assistance in developing this exhibition. Deutsches Haus at New York University, the Goethe-Institut New York, and German Films have also played a critical role in the success of *The Berlin School* at MoMA. My thanks go as well to the individuals and distributors who have lent prints for the exhibition. Finally, thanks are due to Laurence Kardish, former Senior Curator in the Department of Film, for his many decades of involvement with German cinema. His foundational work allows the Museum to present these films in the larger context of German film history.

Glenn D. Lowry
Director, The Museum of Modern Art

Introduction

Rajendra Roy

Angela Schanelec. *Nachmittag* (*Afternoon*). 2007. 35mm film, color, 97 minutes. Production still. Reinhold Vorschneider and Angela Schanelec

The fall of the Berlin Wall triggered a collapse not only of political institutions but also of many elements of German cultural identity, particularly in the former East. Berlin, with its physical borders demolished, became the epicenter of the country's attempts to reintegrate and to progress politically, economically, and culturally. In the mid-1990s a small group of Berlin-based auteur filmmakers emerged, building from what we can see now, twenty years on, was the intellectual rubble of the Wall. The three founding figures of what came to be known as the Berlin School—Thomas Arslan, Christian Petzold, and Angela Schanelec —all studied at the dffb (Deutsche Film- und Fernsehakademie Berlin, the German Film and Television Academy), but their allegiance was to each other as filmmakers, not as members of a collective movement. Indeed, the Berlin School has always been a critics' designation, not an artists' declaration. Its filmmakers are not aggressively political, and their films are not thematically dogmatic; however, many of them strive to provide a cinematic expression of the search for a new German identity (more recently expanded to include other national and cultural geographies). The films often focus on observant characters struggling to adapt in a time of societal change and explore the difficulties of that adaptation. All of the directors are from the former West, but many of the narratives focus on the Easterners, who were more directly affected by the collapse of their society. The Berlin School's signature portrayals of determined and often desperate attempts to inhabit the present tense reject the notion that the most compelling German stories come from its totalitarian past.[1] And even though there are glimmers of optimism about an uncharted future, the films also expose a lingering reluctance to change.

Perhaps most critical for the impact and legacy of the Berlin School films, and the factor that ensures their ongoing relevance, is the keen intellect of their creators. Many of the principal filmmakers are able to articulate their visions both in their films and in their writing. Like the French New Wave, the Berlin School is made up of filmmakers who are also authors, fine artists, and critics. This book, which accompanies the exhibition *The Berlin School: Films from the Berliner Schule*, provides a platform for the filmmakers. Thomas Arslan, Valeska Grisebach, Benjamin Heisenberg, Christoph Hochhäusler, and Christian Petzold all contribute essays, observations, or interviews, adding new chapters to the rich and complex written history of auteur filmmaking in Germany. Given MoMA's earlier in-depth investigations of that history, it is not surprising that a new movement such as the Berlin School would be discussed here in the context of its predecessors—most particularly, the New German Cinema of the 1960s and 1970s. But Hochhäusler challenges easy assumptions about lineage in his essay, "On Whose Shoulders: The Question of Aesthetic Indebtedness" and situates the Berlin School films on a global terrain, noting that filmmakers such as

Abbas Kiarostami, Apichatpong Weerasethakul, and Howard Hawks have been at least as influential on the movement as Fritz Lang, Rainer Werner Fassbinder, or Werner Herzog. This becomes increasingly important to note as the influence of the Berlin School spreads internationally and the kinship with other contemporary auteurs is affirmed.

By illuminating these historical and global links, by investigating the filmmakers' motivations, and by exhibiting a range of their films, our hope is to provide opportunities for an international audience to develop a broader familiarity with the Berlin School. For all its landmark innovations, vital narratives, and powerhouse performances, it has not yet had the exposure it deserves. The Berlin International Film Festival, or Berlinale, has championed these films and directors from their emergence, initially in the Forum, Panorama, and Perspektive sections, followed by the main competition. It remains faithful to the cause, bestowing top awards on directors Ulrich Köhler and Petzold and serving as encouragement to other international festivals—Venice, Toronto, New York, and others—to include them in their selections. Audiences outside the festival circuit began to embrace certain of the films only after the Berlin School had been in existence almost two decades. Most prominent has been Petzold's *Barbara* (2012), a period piece set in 1980s East Germany, starring Nina Hoss. The film was Germany's official submission to the Academy Awards®, a first for a Berlin School director, and it increased the visibility of the movement. At the dffb and other film schools across Western Europe, students now study Berlin School films, much as they have those of the Weimar era and the New German Cinema. Each new filmmaker who engages with the strategies of established Berlin School directors inevitably modifies them, creating new variations on the movement's themes and aesthetics. With this perpetual regeneration, the films of the first generations of the Berlin School will be continually revisited, making it hard to say definitively when the movement, or more importantly its influence, has ended. For now, we are content to witness the full flourishing of what Dennis Lim suggests here is the "Next New Wave."

Notes

1 Concurrent with the emergence of the Berlin School, films such as *Nirgendwo in Afrika* (*Nowhere in Africa*, 2001), *Goodbye Lenin!* (2003), *Der Untergang* (*Downfall*, 2004), and *Das Leben der Anderen* (*The Lives of Others*, 2006) were released. Set in or focused on the aftermath of Germany's totalitarian regimes, these films were commercially successful and won many international awards, something not commonplace with the Berlin School films.

Thomas Arslan. Der schöne Tag (A Fine Day). 2001.
35mm film, color, 74 minutes. Production still. Left to right: Thomas Arslan, Michael Wiesweg, and Theo Lustig

Christian Petzold. Barbara. 2012.
35mm film, color, 105 minutes. Production still. Hans Fromm and Christian Petzold (right)

The Beginning

Anke Leweke

Thomas Arslan. *Mach die Musik leiser* (*Turn Down the Music*). 1994. 35mm film, color, 85 minutes. Left to right: Andy Lehmann, Marco Germund, and Andreas Böhmer

It was a revelation. As if *in* the cinema, my eyes were being opened *by* cinema. You just had to watch and see what was happening on the screen. At a Berlinale screening in the mid-1990s, suddenly there was this group of young people on screen, just graduated from school. Silently lounging around in ice-cream shops, in front of service stations, sitting on walls and railings, waiting for whatever may come. Now and again one takes a drag on a cigarette, sips a soda, or starts a conversation, rarely lasting longer than a couple of exchanges.

> "So what are your plans?"
> "Don't know, hang out for a while, and you?"
> "I'll see."

Not much more actually happened, yet a whole way of being was revealed to me, because the film was taking its dramatic tension from real life. And, at a certain age, didn't we all simply drift for a while, just hanging out? Extending—like the sixteen- and seventeen-year-olds in Thomas Arslan's directorial debut *Mach die Musik leiser* (*Turn Down the Music*, 1994)—the last days of youth into an eternal present, while apprenticeships, jobs, in short: adulthood, were looming on the horizon? Each snapshot contributes to a sense of idling in Arslan's work, which is perhaps the quintessence of youth rather than the spectrum of grand feelings frequently evoked in cinema. In his subsequent Berlin Trilogy, Arslan would again take the viewer along into the reality of German streets, immersing himself into the movements of his characters, bringing us closer to them with each step.

    The second revelation, at the Berlinale in 1996. Screened in the series New German Films was *Das Glück meiner Schwester* (*My Sister's Good Fortune*, 1995), by Angela Schanelec. Here one could only marvel at the freedom with which the director took the time simply to observe her characters. The film is about a man in love with two sisters. The two women are standing in front of a building entrance, talking. About banal things and issues that concern them. About happiness and their ideas of love. Private as the situation is, Berlin is present on the soundtrack as the incessant roar of traffic, as the noise of a metropolis. In her directorial debut, Schanelec's stern, concentrated compositions have already developed a pleasing transparency into the everyday life and inner lives of her heroes and heroines.

    The third revelation. In 1998, at the German-language new directors film festival in Saarbrücken, I saw a screening of Christian Petzold's *Die Beischlafdiebin* (1998; the title can be translated as "postcoital thief"). The film stood out from the rest of the program like an alien object. In precise, confidently composed images, he follows a roughly forty-year-old woman who has become comfortable living a lie, who seems to be in transit through her own life. A shadowy existence in a film noir shot in color. A woman who, like Petzold's later heroines, struggles for what she believes are her dreams (or at least her options) in life.

Three films, three encounters with directors who represent a shift in the landscape of the German film. In the 1990s that landscape was initially dominated by trivial comedies about the personal relationships of yuppie-like characters in the big city. Then, suddenly, cinema began to open up to German ways of living, to generational mind-sets, to the mood of the country as reflected in a kitchen, on the streets of Berlin, or in a parking lot somewhere in the provinces. It was staggering how radically and how uncompromisingly these directors explored the views and perceptions of their characters, and precisely for that reason returned to objectivity.

Thomas Arslan, Christian Petzold, and Angela Schanelec, who write their own screenplays, continue the tradition of German auteur filmmaking, which was thought to have been virtually lost. These three directors found a home with the intrepid and open-minded producers Michael Weber and Florian Koerner von Gustorf and their company Schramm Film. They also found a home among film critics under the handy classification "the Berlin School," though strictly speaking it is not a school at all but an open association of directors with related aesthetics, in discourse with each other. An open community that continues to be joined by younger directors. The only thing shared by its members, with all the differences in their styles, voices, and subject matter, is the fact that all of them have learned their lessons from cinema history. And perhaps it is precisely their passion for the work of their precursors and their colleagues from all over the world, their delight in being able to enter into dialogue with them, their awareness that every image has a precedent, that makes this cinema so formally aware, so intelligent, and so exciting.

Angela Schanelec, *Das Glück meiner Schwester (My Sister's Good Fortune)*, 1995
35mm film, color, 84 minutes. Wolfgang Michael and Anna Bolk

Christian Petzold, *Die Beischlafdiebin*, 1998
16mm film, color, 85 minutes. Constanze Engelbrecht and Wolfram Berger

Christoph Hochhäusler. *Falscher Bekenner (I Am Guilty)*. 2005. Digital video, color, 90 minutes. Constantin von Jascheroff

On Whose Shoulders:
The Question of
Aesthetic Indebtedness

Christoph Hochhäusler

An unwritten rule of the informal movement that critics like to call the Berlin School is that one not generalize about one's colleagues, that one must avoid the expected "we." At the same time, as a "member," I have had to accept being typecast by others, in articles, research papers, and film series that employ this tenuous (in my view) relationship so routinely and so matter of factly that it is impossible to take it personally.

Whenever I have had to speak abroad about the films of this loose grouping—in which there are friendships, to be sure, even collaborations, but no common direction, and certainly no programmatic consensus—I have frequently been confronted with echoes of other German artists. Among the predictable names that have come up in question-and-answer sessions are those of Rainer Werner Fassbinder, Gerhard Richter, Bertolt Brecht, and even the Becher School of photographers. In short: each questioner has dredged up what he already knows about Germany and tried to relate it to the films, and of course such connections can always be fabricated.

A favorite motif in criticism is the notion of a "skipped generation." In this case, the assertion is that film in Germany sank back into artistic insignificance during the Helmut Kohl era, after the auteur tradition had been propagated there in the late 1960s and brought to full flowering by Fassbinder, Werner Herzog, Alexander Kluge, and others, in what became known as the New German Cinema.[1] And now, some decades later, the Berlin School is said to be carrying on the aims of the earlier group. Seductive as such an account may be—I have occasionally resorted to it myself—it illuminates less than it obscures.

But what actually unites us? Whose shoulders are we standing on? Is there such a thing as a common aesthetic origin? In the following, I attempt to provide a few suggestions, without any claim to comprehensiveness and most definitely without having polled my colleagues.

Art is never produced in a vacuum, but the cinema appears to be an especially contingent medium, one that has traditionally been required to reconcile the most contradictory demands, such as art and

commerce. At the same time, the (feature) film is self-referential to the highest degree. Film history forms into fractals, with the same stories told again and again, and again and again, in a similar way, though there appear to be pendulum swings with respect to style. The Neue Sachlichkeit (New Objectivity) of the 1920s and early 1930s was a response to German Expressionism, postwar Italian Neorealism to the "white telephone film" (escapist Italian films of the fascist era, set in high society); the New Wave arose in opposition to France's "Tradition of Quality"; and the Oberhausen Group has contended with "Papa's cinema."[2] And even though this dialectic does violence to the confusions of film history, the "new earnestness" of the Berlin School can be interpreted as a response to the "culture of entertainment" in the West German cinema of the late 1980s, early 1990s.

But this new earnestness also has a great deal to do with altered social coordinates. With reunification, the issue of identity took on new meaning in radically different ways in the East and in the West. Many in the East felt unsettled by what they perceived as an aggressive economic and cultural takeover, and not infrequently they reacted with withdrawal or with *Ostalgie* (nostalgia for the East that was). In the West, the hangover was milder, mostly associated with the question of what was left of the old Bundesrepublik. Berlin became the site of a new beginning, especially for art, but also of suppression, as the East Berlin scene—and most especially the film scene, including the DEFA (Deutsche Film-Aktien-gesellschaft, the state-owned film studio in East Germany)—was brutally pushed aside. Hans-Jürgen Syberberg was met with ridicule and rancor when he suggested that one of Berlin's (three) opera houses be closed and that, in exchange, DEFA be retained as a center of film production. Munich, previously the unchallenged center of West German film, quickly lost its luster, outshone by a new Berlin cinema (Tom Tykwer, Wolfgang Becker, Dani Levy, Detlev Buck) that promised rejuvenation but offered little else.

The Berlin School films of Thomas Arslan, Christian Petzold, and Angela Schanelec (all of whom grew up in the West) were foreign bodies in this landscape. And it is no coincidence that their early works evoke the old Federal Republic in a more or less opaque way. Theirs is an introspective cinema that questions what remains. Christian Petzold's *Die innere Sicherheit* (*The State I Am In*, 2000), a key film for me, is a good example of this. The film tells about former (West German) leftist terrorists who had a hard landing in the post-ideological age. The old currency, the old certainties are no longer valid—and their own daughter proves how petrified and how hollow her parents' "alternative" has been for a long time. Ulrich Köhler's *Bungalow* (2002) also inductively recounts the Kohl era—using the example of a Bartleby figure who refuses everything, even refusal—and the feeling that something has ended but that something new has not yet taken shape.

The seriousness of these films, criticized often enough as humorless or arty, may also have to do with the fact that almost all of us are cinematic late bloomers (and perhaps for that reason zealots as well). Most of us majored in other fields or even practiced other professions before settling on cinema. Angela Schanelec—like Maria Speth—studied acting and worked as an actress. Thomas Arslan majored in German studies; Christian Petzold, German studies and drama. Benjamin Heisenberg studied sculpture; Ulrich Köhler, art, philosophy, and visual communication; and Henner Winckler, also art. Valeska Grisebach majored in philosophy and German studies; Isabelle Stever, mathematics; and I studied architecture. Almost all of us turned to film only later. Accordingly, most of us were past the age of thirty—unusually old by local standards—and more or less set in our ways by the time we made our debut films.

Although I don't know specifics about my colleagues' preferences and role models, I can say that we share a specific relationship to film history. The habit of thinking about film history as a kind of encyclopedia that one can refer to again and again seems to me more decisive than any fondness for the same type of cinema. In a way, the cinema of the Berlin School is unthinkable without the possibility of ranging through all periods and across national borders that has been offered by the DVD. Some films can be thought of as patent rereadings of previous narratives. Petzold's *Yella* (2007), for example, in which films by Herk Harvey (*Carnival of Souls*, 1962) and Harun Farocki (*Nicht ohne Risiko; Nothing Ventured*, 2004) are blended with a short story by Ambrose Bierce ("An Occurrence at Owl Creek Bridge," 1890). Arslan's *Im Schatten* (*In the Shadows*, 2010) could also be mentioned, as an updating of Jean-Pierre Melville's genre films. With some exaggeration, such films could be called metacinema—they are cinematographic palimpsests, deliberately overwriting "sacred" film texts. The change in cinema brought about by the DVD surely deserves closer study, but to my mind what has changed above all is one's distance from film. Ownership of a DVD, as opposed to a film reel, puts one in control by furnishing analytical tools—pause, forward, back, faster, slower, larger, smaller, as well as audio commentaries and so on—and allows one to research aspects of film history in a way possible before only at considerable expense. I suspect that our "Olympus" is, for that reason, more eclectic than that of previous generations, less rigidly oriented along the Hollywood–Paris axis.

As for stylistic influences, recent Asian cinema—in large part made accessible by the DVD—plays an important role, from Abbas Kiarostami to Hsiao-hsien Hou (whom Arslan names as an important influence), from Apichatpong Weerasethakul (on whom all of us are more or less in agreement) to Lav Diaz (an important discovery for Grisebach), from Sang-soo Hong (a key figure for Köhler) to Edward Yang. These are filmmakers for whom the form is political and who, for all their differences, open up the boundaries of narrative by subverting classical tempo, linear narrative, and identifiable pattern. At the same time, American cinema of the "classical" period is an important reference point—John Ford, Howard Hawks, Raoul Walsh, and of course Fritz Lang, Ernst Lubitsch, and Alfred Hitchcock—as a cinema that was created with the self-assurance of a mass medium whose primacy was as yet unchallenged by other media.

Christoph Hochhäusler. *Falscher Bekenner*. 2005. Constantin von Jascheroff

Thomas Arslan. *Der schöne Tag*. 2001. Serpil Turhan

Confident cinema. Our own national influences, I feel, pale by comparison, at least in terms of conscious quotation from, say, the New German Cinema of the 1970s—which does not mean that Fassbinder and Co. play no role. But, in terms of genealogy, I don't think they constitute the main branch.

In fact, the Berlin School, despite what the label suggests, is not a specifically German phenomenon. All over the world there are filmmakers exploring related terrain. In Austria (Jessica Hausner), in Argentina (Lisandro Alonso, Lucrecia Martel), in the United States (Lance Hammer, Kelly Reichardt), in Japan (Naomie Kawase, Hirokazu Kore-eda), and in many other places. But just what is this terrain? I feel it would be mistaken to focus on formal decisions, such as long takes. More important, it seems to me, is a certain approach to narrative and a specific concept of characters, both of which have formal consequences. I am sure that each of us would describe these shared approaches differently or even dispute them altogether, but it is my sense that three factors play a paramount role.

First, in terms of narrative, there is a shift away from the center and toward the periphery. In nineteenth-century history painting, the idea was to depict the decisive instant, the very moment that Caesar crossed the Rubicon. By contrast, French Impressionism focused on the beauty of the quotidian, and the historic moment was disregarded. One can interpret the shift that distinguishes our films from the American mainstream or from its offshoots in German television drama in just this way. Instead of the decisive moment, for us it is more a matter of before or after, and seldom is the main character a figure who "makes history." Rather—and now we come to my second factor—it is about characters who stand at the periphery of events, with interior lives the viewer can only speculate about. Perhaps this could be called antiexhibitionism; by no means are all the figures timid or mute, but none of them pretends to be as self-congratulatory as the heroes we are accustomed to from the mainstream. One could also say that the characters preserve their mystery, and with it their dignity. It is therefore not surprising that the majority of our characters are adolescents, young people who are more observers than protagonists. This leads to the third factor—a cinema of observation, not of action. It is not plot entanglements that are most important,

but rather the vision, the view of the world. This is ideally realized in Schanelec's *Marseille* (2004), in which a photographer, played by Maren Eggert, "surrenders herself to the [strange] city"[3] in order to become a witness rather than an active participant. In this, we link up with a long tradition in the European cinema, from F. W. Murnau to Andrei Tarkovsky, from Michelangelo Antonioni to Robert Bresson.

The question of how German our films are has led to controversy again and again, especially given the elective affinities with filmmakers outside Germany. Aside from the love for the language, there are few things German that we worship; there is not much flag-waving going on among us. Our films speak of the here and now, to be sure, and many of them are set in the German provinces. But when asked, most Berlin School directors describe themselves as European or see themselves—at least on the cinema map—as cosmopolitan. What links us perhaps more strongly than issues of national identity are German production conditions. And here a paradox comes into play that is either sad or comical, depending on how you look at it. The films of the Berlin School—which are committed to cinema as a space for concentration, where a storyteller can trust the audience to register subtle signs, in contrast to the crude antics of television drama—find their largest (though still modest) audiences on television. There are both structural and cultural reasons for this. Among the structural reasons is the fact that we do not have a film industry per se but rather a (predominantly public) television industry on which producers depend as well as various public funding institutions. However, cinema is little more than a showcase for television, a "flagship store" as Harun Farocki put it,[4] that at best lends prestige to its programming.

True commercial success in German cinema is a rare exception; the rule is the exploitation of cinema as window dressing in television programming. Accordingly, the same people are found both in front of and behind the camera both in cinema and in television, which further blurs the distinction between the mediums. On top of this come cultural factors. Traditionally, film has earned no particular respect as art in Germany; whereas music, theater, and the fine arts all enjoy great prestige, the cinema is still seen as mere entertainment. As a result, our films are made on very limited budgets, which is inevitably apparent in the

Ulrich Köhler. *Montag kommen die Fenster (Windows on Monday)*. 2006. 35mm film, color, 88 minutes. Isabelle Menke

Christoph Hochhäusler. *Milchwald (This Very Moment)*. 2003. Digital video, color, 87 minutes. Judith Engel

finished product and influences the choice of material, the number of roles, and the film's design. A large part of this economy of means, which is often celebrated and at least as often reviled, is thus simply … economy. Or the result of it. We have learned to love the "aesthetic of poverty." Because it is wise to love what is possible? That would be too pessimistic, but it is not altogether beside the point.

Even if we do not share a manifesto, as I mentioned above, we are in constant dialogue with each other. Not everyone with everyone else, but it is a lively association. There are also obvious collaborations. A handful of cameramen (Reinhold Vorschneider, Bernhard Keller, Patrick Orth, Hans Fromm), casting directors (Simone Bär, Nina Haun, Ulrike Müller), editors (Bettina Böhler, Stefan Stabenow), and production designers (Silke Fischer, Kade Gruber, Renate Schmaderer, Beatrice Schultz) have been involved in a majority of our films. A few directors share writing credits—recently, for example, Henner Winckler and Ulrich Köhler on *I Turn to You* (forthcoming). Benjamin Heisenberg cowrote my debut film, *Milchwald* (*This Very Moment*, 2003), and Valeska Grisebach served as Maren Ade's dramatic advisor for *Alle Anderen* (*Everyone Else*, 2009)—to name some examples.

That many films are consequently made "in close proximity, without fences" as Christian Petzold put it[5] —that is to say, with repeated references to one another—is hardly surprising. I felt Petzold's *Gespenster* (*Ghosts*, 2005), for example, to be to some extent a reaction to Schanelec's *Marseille* (2004): a French couple in Berlin, two young women lost in their own city. My second feature film, *Falscher Bekenner* (*I Am Guilty*, 2005), was in many respects conceived as a response to Köhler's debut, *Bungalow* (2002). In Ulrich's film, the hero seemed rootless, which is why I made a family film. And also Köhler's *Montag kommen die Fenster* (*Windows on Monday*, 2006) could be understood as an (unconscious) alternative take on my *Milchwald*, in that it also deals with a woman who neglects her maternal duties and flees her unfinished house. Many other such connections could be made. Films criticize films, build upon visual experiences, continue narratives, reformulate ideas. The same is true in Hollywood, but in our case it takes place on a more intimate scale.

The picture would not be complete if I failed to mention formative teachers and mentors. Arslan, Petzold, and Schanelec found Hartmut Bitomsky and Harun Farocki to be important teachers at the dffb (Deutsche Film- und Fernsehakademie Berlin, the German Film and Television Academy) and even got to know each other in their seminars. As students, Petzold and Arslan assisted Bitomsky and Farocki on various projects, and to this day Farocki collaborates on Petzold's screenplays. He also served as dramatic advisor on Isabelle Stever's upcoming project, *Hotel Lounge*. This connection with Farocki and Bitomsky is surely the most telling proof of the theory of the "skipped generation" (which I rejected above). But it is no coincidence that the two men were by no means protagonists of the New German Cinema but rather antagonists, first as writers and editors of the important journal *Filmkritik*, then in their documentary works (and also in the failure of their feature-film experiments intended to counter the literary adaptations then in vogue). Their films and analytical methods have left perhaps their clearest traces on the Berlin School—at least, on its "first generation." But even among younger members there have been formative encounters with filmmakers of that earlier generation, all of them New German Cinema outsiders who turned to teaching partly in response to the precarious working conditions. Köhler and Winckler, for example, found teachers and champions in the experimental filmmakers Rüdiger Neumann and Klaus Wyborny. Important for me was Tankred Dorst, known mainly as a dramatist, who in the late 1970s–early 1980s made three very personal and unjustly forgotten films with a keen sense of German history and "disruptive people"[6] —*Klaras Mutter* (*Clara's Mother*, made for television, 1978); *Mosch* (1980, also made for TV); *Eisenhans* (*Strange Fruits*, 1983)—and who occasionally reads my screenplays even today.

"The Berlin School" is a critics' label. Originally coined to describe the cinema of Arslan, Petzold, and Schanelec, it gradually came to encompass a great many other directors, including me. Because each critic counts differently and identifies different stylistic features as typical, various subsets have been identified. It is important to recognize that such designations fail to fully accommodate all its "members" and their works. That was true ten years ago, and it is even truer now. Every label carries an expiration date, and to my mind this one has passed. The films of the last few years have veered further and further apart. Genre and costume films, comedies, and thrillers have tended more and more to defy expectations, a development that I find both necessary and liberating. School is out, and I am eager to see what comes next.

Notes

1 In 1962 a group of cinephiles—among them Alexander Kluge, Edgar Reitz, Peter Schamoni, and Herbert Vesely—declared their "ambition to create the new German feature film." This so-called Oberhausen Manifesto positioned itself against the dying UFA tradition and cleared the way for the New German Cinema, even if most of the signatories (with the exception of Kluge and Reitz) failed to ride the wave they helped to create. See http://www. oberhausener-manifest.com/oberhausener-manifest/.
2 The radical young filmmakers of the Oberhausen Group declared that "Papas Kino ist tot" (Papa's cinema is dead).
3 Schanelec wrote in the press material for the release of the film: "A young photographer travels to Marseille. The more she becomes fixated with the city, the harder it becomes for her to return to her former life. She must deal with the consequences." See http://www.peripherfilm.de/marseille/inhalt.htm.
4 Interview with Harun Farocki, "Zukunft Kino," *Kinema Kommunal* (magazine of the Bundesverband Kommunale Filmarbeit e.V.) 1 (January–March 2008): 2.
5 Petzold has used this expression many times in conversation. See, for example, our email exchange in Dominik Graf, Christian Petzold, and Christoph Hochhäusler, "Mailwechsel Berliner Schule," *Revolver* 16 (May 2007): 9, where he says: "Perhaps the whole business of the Berlin School has something to do with it. That one didn't have a supportive environment, that the films also had no context, nothing to be compared to. The same thing is surely behind your desire for genre, after all, for genre means context, tradition, deviations and conformities. I happen to like our present loose relationship, or community without fences."
6 Dorst, from an interview with his cowriter Ursula Ehler, *Revolver* 18 (January 5, 2008): 60–87. Ehler described their films as being about people who "are in the way."

Top and bottom: Christoph Hochhäusler, *Milchwald*, 2003. Leonard Bruckmann and Sophie Charlotte Conrad

Christian Petzold. *Barbara*. 2012. 35mm film, color, 105 minutes. Production still. Nina Hoss and Christian Petzold

French Cancan in the DDR:
An Exchange with Christian Petzold

Anke Leweke

Again and again in Christian Petzold's films there are scenes that stand alone, that at first glance have nothing to do with the story. In his film Barbara *(2012), about a doctor who wants to escape from East Germany (the DDR), such a scene takes place in a popular restaurant where the title character has met a messenger from her West German lover. Suddenly her gaze, and ours, falls on a group of waitresses lying on the floor with their legs up.*

Once people have made the life decision to leave their country, they perceive their surroundings only very selectively. The doctor Barbara has had it with the DDR and wants to flee. Now her senses are numbed. She no longer experiences the country in any detail, in any of its contradictions. But all the things that happen in this film are things she can no longer classify. She gazes out the train window and sees a group of young men on motorcycles, dressed in colorful clothes. They wave at the train—an affirmation of life that doesn't match Barbara's image of the DDR.

My grandmother had a restaurant in the DDR. Once when we visited her, we ate in another restaurant because she wanted to see how other people cooked and ran their places. There, just as in the film, we saw a group of waitresses resting their legs against the wall. My grandmother explained that it was good for varicose veins. That scene suddenly came back to me. Barbara comes into the restaurant with the sole intention of arranging for the money for her escape. That is all told simply—as clearly as in American cinema, without detours or ambiguity. Then suddenly she sees these young women lying on the floor, chatting with each other, their skirts pulled up, their naked legs. The women are at peace with themselves, concerned about their health, off duty. We called the scene "the Cancan of the DDR," because it looked as if they were about to dance with their skirts lifted high. These things are important for the Barbara character, because she suddenly recognizes that the DDR has its charms after all, that the country offers things she may have overlooked.

Something else resonates in this scene. In the West we were always convinced that people in the DDR only wanted to come across, that there was no life there. But the "Cancan" tells another story. When Barbara plays the piano, for example, it is Chopin, and with it an allusion to the old historical and cultural ties between Poland and France. So there's the suggestion of a westward yearning that goes beyond the capitalistic Bundesrepublik. A longing for a country with culture, where even as a foreigner a person can fit in. Beyond the escape and the journey that will

take her to Düsseldorf, where her lover lives, there is still another West, and that is actually Barbara's pipe dream.

Barbara and the wind, a story of longing. The wind comes from the sea, across which Barbara wants to flee. But for a long time you don't see the sea. You only feel the wind from the coast.

Cinema has to show me the visible world! That's not only a metaphorical wind. Of course, it's also the wind of history, of revolt, the wind of aggression, but essentially it's simply the wind. When the wind is physical and sensual and doesn't yet carry a sense of the sea, then it is suddenly music, then it is suddenly a resistance, then it is suddenly something beautiful. You see how it plays in the leaves, the hair, and it's sensational if you can film that. There aren't a lot of camerapeople who can do it, because it's of no interest to them. Because it's only the face that matters, and what the face sees. That the facial expression is influenced and impressed by what it sees—that is what you're supposed to film.

FROM THE EAST TO THE WILD WEST

Yella (2007)—a woman from the East searches for happiness and money in the West. She finds a job with an investment shark and his private equity firm. She lives with him in anonymous hotels, learns the deceptions of the trade, makes deals in featureless offices. It is an excursion into the immaterial world of money, in which a woman tries to reinvent herself.

I had read Marc Augé's fantastic essay "Non-Places."[1] Like all great philosophers—Hegel or Marx, for example—he can tell stories. It became clear to me why we like modern finance capitalism. There must be something to it, or it would never have triumphed. Augé describes a modern man who arrives at the airport, surrenders his bag (which holds only a shirt), and keeps his jacket, in which are his ticket, his Visa card, and his cell phone. He goes through check-in, is X-rayed, and arrives at the boarding area, feeling strangely free because he has no responsibility, no baggage. He has discarded all his ballast—indeed, to an extent unprecedented in the history of mankind. He can pay everywhere with his credit cards. The only thing that upsets him on his flight is that he can't order any alcohol when flying through Saudi Arabian airspace. Marc Augé also

writes that when we drive on French freeways, to the right and left are the loveliest châteaux, but we can no longer see them through the sound barricades. Such is our modern world. We no longer take part in it in a sensual way; it is only quoted. And this image of the traveler without ballast—that's what has to be shown. That's what Yella likes. It's by no means a matter of balance sheets anymore. She sits next to this man, her boss, and the business becomes a game. For all the horrors of finance capitalism, you also have to tell about the fascination of this world.

Yella is the last part of the Gespenster (*Ghosts*) *Trilogy. In* Die innere Sicherheit (*The State I Am In, 2000) and* Gespenster (*2005*), *the characters already seem like phantoms. Or like transients in the waiting rooms of their own histories or of our common history. The phantom as the modern figure of the cinema.*

What worries me is the outsourcing of work. Outsourced from the hearts of the industrial nations because we are dominated by finance capitalism. But work is what keeps us from becoming phantoms. At least there is still handwork. At least there's the possibility of objectifying, of seeing oneself, as in Marx, represented by something you've made. If you build a bridge,

you can drive there with your children and show it to them. Or tell them you were the structural engineer. That's a job. But for us, work has disappeared. For that reason, the number of phantoms has increased. The ghosts that haunt employment agencies. Ghosts because they only provide services or sit in front of computers. And also, there are only ghostly conditions, because everything that made up the working class, the trade unions, has disappeared. "All the wheels stop still if our strong arm so wills" [a line from the anthem written for the General Association of German Workers in 1863]. All that has been destroyed.

We are experiencing the destruction of social space by the outsourcing of work to places we know nothing about. So we're totally shocked if nine-year-olds are sewing our shirts. But work is identity, and if there's no longer identity, the number of phantoms increases. And I feel that the history of film is filled with people on the verge of becoming phantoms. Who try to define themselves in terms of money (which is a mistake), or the search for happiness, or criminality, or love. And to trace this search for meaning in cinema is political.

WORK FLOW I

Again and again, Christian Petzold films his phantoms from behind, following them as they try to step out from the world of shadows into the real world. Covering their backs.

Every approach to narrative produces its own shots. If you move along in front of the characters, they walk for the camera, and you clear the way for them. If you follow them, after twenty yards they forget the camera. As observers, we see people moving through the world, so we have to move through the world with them, have to follow them. They're not following us. And when we follow people, we're more observant.

Christian Petzold. *Yella*. 2007. Production still. Nina Hoss, Hans Fromm (looking into camera), and Matthias Kapinos (right)

FROM SHORT FILM TO SHORT STORY

Jerichow (2008)—A Turkish businessman in the German East. His wife, who doesn't love him but feels financially dependent on him. A soldier returned from the war in Afghanistan. A triangle in inhospitable surroundings. An outing to the sea. A scene that stands on its own like a short story.

You see a man, filmed against the sea, listening to Turkish music. The man is virtually beside himself. He's drunk, and creating for himself a bridge to Turkey. Across the sea, across the music, and across the alcohol, he sets out on a journey of homesickness. Like a kind of Icarus. He's full of vitality and longing.

And the next step is the two people crouched nearby. A man and a woman who have not yet clarified their relationship observe the man. They are jealous. Jealous because they suddenly see something about themselves, their lousy debts, their lousy money, their botched German lives. Here's a man who at this moment is happy. And what does the other man say? "You dance like a Greek." He means like Zorba. Out of sheer viciousness, to confront the Turk with a different self-image, to destroy him. And something like that delights me, when all that is there in a little scene. When all that is going on under the surface, when the resentments, meanness, and perfidy are felt. And the people in the picture are ashamed of their baseness but nonetheless can't help themselves.

Much the same happens in Heinrich von Kleist's essay "On the Marionette Theater," when somebody tells the narcissist that he swims incredibly beautifully. "You swim just like in such and such a painting." And immediately the narcissist is faced with

an image that shatters him. He can never again swim the way he swam before, simply for himself, because he had not seen himself reflected before. The image, the reflection, destroys him.

A charged scene that already contains the relationships between the characters, perhaps even the entire story. One could list other such scenes, describe them, analyze them. But how do they make up a film?

When I work with Harun Farocki [the director who was Christian Petzold's teacher, and continues to be his mentor and advisor], we create variations on one primal scene, just as when composing music. But always with the same people in the same spaces. The production directors say: "That won't be so expensive at all." And I reply: "Wrong. It will be expensive, because we won't be shooting chronologically." We leave the site, film something, then return later. We don't film them all in sequence, because the variation, the difference from scene to scene, is what actually constitutes the story.

Something is hidden in this crucial scene that is not yet altogether clear to me. Something that is also found in American short stories, also in Guy de Maupassant and Anton Chekhov. The situations open up a space and immediately close it again. As if they had only opened the windows and a breeze has stirred the static relationships. And no more can be interpreted. For that reason, the moment in which the interpretation, the literature reach their limits is the one in which the cinema begins. The same thing happens in the short story, otherwise it would have become a novel. That's why you can't film novels. Novels obey different rules; they are literary and have no need of cinema.

Top and bottom: Christian Petzold. *Gespenster*. 2005. Benno Fürmann.

WORK FLOW II

Christian Petzold wants to make you apprehend the world through his framing of reality, not through specific images or symbols. Compressing the world into a picture frame.

When two people talk to each other, they create their own space. But the space surrounding them is nonetheless still there, too—

otherwise, this self-created space is not sufficiently powerful, and it remains simply a stage. In a club, then, where the music is pounding, two people gaze into each other's eyes and for a moment no longer hear the music and no longer have any sense of their surroundings—that's what we have to see. To describe their space as well as the objective space that carries on without them, that's what is interesting.

ON THE ROAD

Youth on the run. In Die innere Sicherheit, *the adolescent Jeanne is riding in a car through southern Europe and Germany with her parents, a pair of leftist terrorists who have gone underground. The camera brings the outside world, the world the girl longs for, into the car.*

The girl sits in the back. It's a family bubble inside the Volvo; as in a Faraday cage, you're protected from the lightning, but at the same time you feel as if you're imprisoned. Now if I had moved from Julia Hummer, from her close-up, to the outside, and if we had seen Hamburg or Wuppertal sweeping by, I would have found that cruel. For we mustn't show the girl's yearning through pictures; the yearning is in her gaze. That's why we don't see what she's looking at—she sees things that are hers alone. And we show only her gaze. That's what I explained to everybody: we don't have any point-of-view shots.

That's also why we shoot in an actual moving car and not on a trailer or in the studio. Because I don't want the world to get any shots of its own, even though it is out there. It flies by outside, the places where we filmed, the fields or even the cities or the intersections. They're not arbitrary, they've been carefully chosen. But they don't get shots of their own, because I find it presumptuous to film a girl's point of view there.

ON THE ROAD: THE AUTOMOBILE AND GERMAN SOCIETY

To me the automobile has two meanings, which is why it played a role even in my first film. *Pilotinnen* (*Pilots*, 1995) was a pure road movie. On the one hand, because for Germany everything revolved around the automobile, and still does, even though it won't much longer. At the same time, this car never actually appears in the stories, although Germans spend more time behind the steering wheel than in front of the television set. There's a whole industry that caters to these people. Radio programs, audio dramas, audiobooks. Great German actors read important world literature for automobile drivers. This stuff lies around in their cars. People have created little hideaways in their cars, like fantasy spaces, spaces in which they go on journeys along freeways and highways. Lots of people also head for their cars in order to find peace. And the car is antisocial, because the driver sees only himself and the world through the windshield. That in itself is a cinema world, an imaginary world. A fiction.

Christian Petzold. *Wolfsburg*. 2003. 16mm film blown up to 35mm, color, 90 minutes, Nina Hoss

The second thing: German actors in television and also in cinema are constantly pressed into stagy situations, so that they are really acting everywhere. But you can't do that in a car. The car is the most antitheatrical place there is. And as for the car, you can hardly capture the whole situation inside. Only with shot and countershot. That's not possible in the theater, is itself antitheater. In the car the actors are only bust-length figures, and they don't have to talk loudly. They're very close to each other. They have no fourth wall, they're surrounded by the world. And if the actors don't see the car as a stage, but as a means of transportation in actual traffic, I have noticed that they take delight in that and suddenly speak differently. They have a different posture, use different gestures, do much less with their facial expressions. For in the car every glance or gaze to the side, each smile is a sensation.

ON THE ROAD: THE AUTOMOBILE AND THE GERMAN LEFT

The German Autumn [the period in September and October 1977 when the Red Army Faction carried out a series of terrorist attacks] was the first death struggle for the Left; the second was the collapse of the DDR. Then they could no longer stand capitalism's orgy of jubilation, they literally had to hide from it. I noticed this once I had children myself: how the Left bought itself houses and land, built up its own networks, health-food stores, day-care centers, whole-grain bakeries—the whole alternative culture became more and more a gated community. That was no longer politics but retreat to an island: "I'm not going along with your shit, but we're no longer changing the world either." To me, the white Volvo was the right car for this. I drive cautiously, but if somebody runs into me I'll survive. That's why I chose to use a Volvo in *Die innere Sicherheit*—I don't want to represent anything or have anything to do with the fascist German auto industry.

WORK FLOW III

We always travel to all the locations, whether constructed, historical, or simply available ones. And I spend two days there with the actors, staying overnight; we simply sit there, smoking and drinking and getting our bearings, and I tell them why I chose the place, and of course they also ask me, "Why here?" And then

I have to share my thinking, lay my cards on the table, which I like to do. Naturally, there is also a directorial style that keeps its thoughts to itself. But I find that communicating leads to more ideas. You have to have discussed the sensuality or nonsensuality, the fiction or nonfiction of the locations. They thereby stock their tool kits and pack their bags for the coming job.

Christian Petzold. *Yella*. 2007. Production still. Nina Hoss and Christian Petzold

THE ETERNAL FRICTION

*The New German Cinema introduced a new and diverse discourse
around (previously suppressed) German history. In Berlin School
cinema, new, contemporary frictions appear: social upheavals
following the fall of the Wall, the effects of the new capitalism.
And nonetheless…*

I can't get away from fascism, as I see so much of it in the present,
deal with finance capitalism. The years from 1933 to 1945 are and
always will be a tremendous burden.

I was born in 1960, started school in 1966, and graduated in
1979. In fact, one could say that I was blessed by being born very
late. But the anti-Semitism of the Left, the old and new Nazis, the
deep hatred of Jews that still exists in Germany. Perhaps for that
reason I want to deal with it in my next film, which will be set in
the postwar period. Although one shouldn't look into the heart of
darkness.

This year the Berlinale featured the retrospective series
The Weimar Touch. Those films showed once again which directors
had to emigrate and the world view they took with them.

Since then, we no longer have any narrative of our own.
I find that we have no comedies, only sketches. That we have no
idea of culture, are always merely educational. We're a nation
of offenders, after all, as if for that reason we have no need for
a cinema that can venture onto dubious, fascinating, dangerous
terrain. When I see what was shattered at that time and has never
returned, I still find that the Federal Republic's greatest wound,
in every respect. That's why I have to live in Berlin, because here
you're faced with the wound every day.

Notes

1 Marc Augé, *Non-lieux: Introduction à une anthropologie de la surmodernité*
(Paris: Éditions du Seuil, 1992).

Angela Schanelec. *Plätze in Städten (Places in Cities)*. 1998. 35mm film, color, 117 minutes. Sophie Aigner

Women's Lab:
The Female Protagonist
in the Berlin School

Rajendra Roy

In late 2005 Angela Merkel was first elected chancellor of Germany. Raised in the former East Germany, she was the youngest person elected to that position since World War II, the first born in the postwar era, the first scientist (a quantum chemist by training), and the first woman. It had been fifteen years since the beginning of reunification and less than a decade since the seat of government moved back to Berlin. I was working in Berlin, as the only non-European member of the selection committee for the Berlinale, and I asked one of my colleagues—a film critic, curator, and by all readings, politically left-leaning—how he felt about the newly elected conservative government and its leader. He responded without hesitation: "It's time Germany was led by a woman." Did her gender matter more than her politics, or was it merely the moment for change? Top political leadership in Germany had always been in the hands of men. Could an empowered woman assert a more effective new form of authority? Or was it rather that a woman would be less evocative of the sinister leaders that have marked German history?

Internationally, Merkel has become emblematic of reunified Germany's authoritative (mostly economic) rise in Europe. Internally, however, her ascension is seen more as an anomaly than as announcing a new reality for women. If anything, she seems to represent the conflicted and (particularly in the former East) untethered state of post-Wall Germany. With an array of factors in play from the different political, social, and economic spheres and with the distinct cultural traditions specific to East and West contrasting with the elements they share, the nation has become a laboratory for identities in flux.

Insights into fluctuating identity and the role that women could play in interpreting and shaping it have emerged in the work of the Berlin School filmmakers, who are a remarkably equal mix of women and men. Collectively, they investigate from different angles the merging of East and West, male and female roles in society, the nature of authority, and capitalism and its pitfalls—all set against Germany's complex political history. The protagonists of these directors' narratives are almost invariably women. Some are presented as blank slates, liberated but not yet able to fully harness and direct their power; others struggle to set a new course. All of them provoke questions.

MOTION

Starting a process requires motion, whether caused by a reaction or by an independent impulse. In a society attempting to define its purpose anew, the temptation may be to shun the past, but that only makes it more likely that the past will inform the future. This can lead to a profound sense of being stuck, both collectively and personally. One strategy to regain mobility is to break a life down to the basic, even mundane, elements of existence, then scrutinize the traditional purpose of those elements and, if necessary, reconfigure them. The work of Angela Schanelec demonstrates how this can be achieved cinematically. She pioneered and perfected techniques that are now identified as signatures of the Berlin School. By extending her characters' conversations beyond the traditional boundaries of plot and narrative, she desentimentalizes domestic life, drilling into its deeper meaning and exposing raw truths. She rejects musical scores, instead using local sound and in situ music in order to evoke a space rather than a state of mind. Her brilliant collaborations with the cinematographer Reinhold Vorschneider bring a luminosity to her pictures that belie their mundane scenarios. These strategies have been embraced by a preponderance of Berlin School directors, who have inflected their own films with nuanced variations on them.

In *Plätze in Städten* (*Places in Cities*, 1998), Schanelec opens the film cold, on a seemingly commonplace, inconsequential breakup scene. What makes it nontraditional (at least in the context of popular cinema) is that we see a passive, browbeaten man (Mischa Sideris) pleading with an empowered young woman (Sophie Aigner). She is viewed only from the back, withholding her face from us, her no-nonsense ponytail at the center of the frame:

"I'm going now," she says.

"You can't do that."

"Yes." She's in a bad mood and makes an excuse for needing to leave.

"I'll come along. I'll watch you. I'm in love with you. I'll sit down, smoke and watch you. You can think about other things. I won't touch you. I'm making a fool of myself, but I don't care. I won't kiss you. I won't touch you."

He attempts to regain his footing but ultimately recognizes that she holds all the cards, that she will liberate him from their love affair, and he is lost.

"Sometimes it's good to be a fool. To realize that you are a fool and not care a bit. You don't understand that, do you? Do you understand me?"

"It doesn't matter."

"So you do understand me, of course you understand me. But I don't understand anything. . . . Someday you'll beg to be understood. Not yet, but someday for sure. Then you can call me . . ."

"Good, I'll call."

"I'll be an old man."

Maren Ade. *Der Wald vor lauter Bäumen* (*The Forest for the Trees*). 2003. Digital video, color, 81 minutes. Eva Löbau

Maria Speth. *In den Tag hinein*. 2001. Sabine Timoteo and Hiroki Mano

This exchange establishes the assumption of personal authority that will propel Schanelec's story of the young woman's investigation of place and belonging. The young woman may not yet know her future, but she knows it is no longer with him. He is the status quo, and she is the uncharted way forward. Schanelec further examines the possibility of movement through fixed spaces in her subsequent films. In *Orly* (2010), set in the Paris airport of the same name, the potential for progress (physical and relational) is all around. The question is: Where would people go if they could get there?

In director Maren Ade's feature debut, *Der Wald vor lauter Bäumen* (*The Forest for the Trees*, 2003), another young woman, Melanie (Eva Löbau), embodies progress, and in this case she has a vision of what her future is, or at least what it should be. Shot with a handheld digital video camera, the film has the look and feel of a low-budget documentary, with all of the incumbent rawness and urgency. Determined to establish a better life for herself and her community, the slightly awkward Melanie moves away from her family and her lethargic boyfriend to teach a new generation in a new town in the German provinces. Her idealism is battered by the unwillingness of the members of that close-knit society to accept her optimistic overtures (as odd and off-putting as they may be) and by the real cruelty just below the surface in the people around her. When stymied by their pervasive rejection of change, she must confront her own naïveté and loss of direction.

Maria Speth explores similar reasons for pessimism in her debut, *In den Tag hinein* (*The Days Between*, 2001), though she shifts the focus of her heroine's struggle from her social surroundings to her own psyche. Lynn (Sabine Timoteo) has no concern for her community or even her family. She despises their bourgeois existence and is determined to thrust herself along a new path blazed by her own fierce volition. A dancer in a disco at night, she works in a cafeteria by day. Her boyfriend is a professional swimmer who spends his days in the same pool going nowhere fast. Just a means of sexual gratification for her, he is ruthlessly dismissed whenever he fails in that service. A Japanese student offers an exotic way out of the mundane, but Lynn is bound to her situation, and reality crashes into her in the end. In a way, she is a classic cinematic rebel, a drifter stifled by the modern middle-class way of life. As that lifestyle came to prevail in the post-Wall era, the only way for a rebel to survive was to stay in motion.

Christian Petzold. *Die innere Sicherheit* (*The State I Am In*). 2000. 35mm film, color, 106 minutes. Julia Hummer

ECONOMIES

Christian Petzold also has an affinity for characters in motion, though in his films they are often unwilling participants in their own journeys.[1] His first cinematic feature, *Die innere Sicherheit* (*The State I Am In*, 2000, cowritten with his teacher and regular collaborator, Harun Farocki), is an anguished tale of the attempt by a disoriented post–Cold War generation to break from inherited history. A teenage girl, Jeanne (Julia Hummer), lives in southern Europe in hiding with her parents. They are fugitives, possible ex–Red Army Faction militants, exiled from the German homeland they had once fought to free from American imperialism and internal repression after World War II. To Jeanne, her parents and the repercussions of their former lives are an ever-increasing impediment to a fulfilling life of her own. Attached to their history, she cannot progress as a young person in society, can't have a boyfriend, buy new clothes, develop social bonds, be "normal." As their lives crumble under the weight of the past, she struggles to participate in a future that has, in many ways, embraced the most American of ideals—bourgeois capitalism.

Petzold follows the thread of capitalism throughout his films, helping to illuminate the aftermath of the clash between West and East, capitalism and communism. As the vanquisher, Capitalism and his strongest offspring, Consumerism, became dominant forces in a reunified Germany. Big-box stores now dot the former East German countryside, and malls occupy the center of rebuilt Berlin. Petzold's film *Gespenster* (*Ghosts*, 2005) is set in and around Potsdamer Platz, the sparkling and sprawling business, shopping, and entertainment district built on the former no-man's-land between East and West. Tourists can have their picture taken (for a fee, of course) with slabs of the Wall where it once stood. His heroine is Nina (Julia Hummer), a nearly adult orphan who can't get out of the social support system that has become her prison. His antiheroine is Toni (Sabine Timoteo). Nina witnesses Toni being attacked in a park but is too timid to intervene. She finds what she believes is Toni's earring on the ground and seeks her out. In truth, Toni is a petty thief, stealing anything she needs (jewels, clothes, hearts) to get though life. Simultaneously leveraging and subverting the system, she spends her life chasing rich guys, auditioning for "reality" shows, and shoplifting in malls. Nina offers a way out, something real and nonconformist in the loving sexual desire she has for Toni. But Toni is addicted to being on the make. It defines her, and she cannot divorce herself from her desire to game the system. Nina is trapped on the inside and Toni on the outside. A French woman enters the picture, trancelike, looking for the daughter, the future, she lost to a kidnapper many years ago, in a shopping center. Her story weaves in and out of the two young women's lives and offers the false hope of a maternal rescue by the previous generation.

The fascination of the West-born Berlin School directors with female protagonists from the former East reflects the more profound cultural impact that reunification had on the East and, particularly, on the women there. "You read in the newspapers of the East that there are no young women anymore," Petzold notes. "The women leave first, not the men; the men are conservative."[2] His remarkably prescient film *Yella* (2007) broadens the scope of the West's individualist victory over the East and its collective approach to progress. Nina Hoss, Petzold's muse and for many the face of the Berlin School, plays the title character: a recently divorced woman from the former East who is thrilled by the opportunity to move west and become an accountant in a large transnational company. As she bids farewell to her countryside home, she is stalked by her former husband, who claims she is abandoning him because of his failure to launch a successful business. She agrees to let him drive her to the train station, where she will board a westbound train. But he takes a detour and steers the car off a bridge into the Elbe River, the former divide between East and West. Yella emerges, disheveled and disoriented, then makes her way to the station and to Hannover, where her new life awaits. The promised job is no more, however, the casualty of a thieving, corrupt, and lecherous boss. She encounters a fellow traveler (much of the film is set in an anonymous corporate hotel), who engages her to accompany him on pitch meetings with potential clients for whom he is brokering loans. Naturally, he too is a thief, gaming the system to enrich himself. She learns quickly, and

Christian Petzold. *Gespenster (Ghosts)*. 2005. 35mm film, color, 85 minutes. Sabine Timoteo and Julia Hummer (right)

Christian Petzold. *Gespenster*. 2005. Sabine Timoteo

perhaps too well, the ways of ruthless capitalism, and in the end she destroys the lives of her clients and the fantasy of her own new existence.

If Yella can be seen as a stand-in for the migratory ambitions of former East Germans, previously isolated from the culture of capitalism, then her downfall does not bode well for those who embrace that culture. Petzold's most successful film to date, *Barbara* (2012), is a period piece set in 1980s East Germany, also starring Nina Hoss. Though set in the communist past, its vivid images of the final throes of a corrupt system have resonated with contemporary audiences. At the film's premiere in Berlin, Petzold responded to Greek journalists who asked if his film was an allegory for contemporary European nations facing their own financial downfall. "I think there is a connection which I didn't think about when I made the movie: that that's also a feeling in Germany and Spain and Greece and Italy—that something in the neo-liberal capitalist system is dying."[3] No doubt the journalists were hoping that Merkel, the woman who had best "succeeded" in migrating from the East to the heights of Western capitalism, was taking heed of Petzold's cautionary tale.

MOTHER LAND

If, as in *Plätze in Städten* and *Die innere Sicherheit*, women characters carry the embryo of a post-Wall German identity, perhaps they truly are the mothers of a present-tense individuality that is just beginning to announce itself. Several Berlin School films have mothers as central or pivotal characters, representing vastly divergent states of being. Petzold's perpetually grieving mother from *Gespenster* is an apparition in search of a phantom child. She symbolizes an ephemeral (European) past, desperately searching for her likeness in the present, denying the reality of irrevocable change. She is more than

just a tragic figure, though; with no progeny to carry on her legacy, she also represents a clean break, a potentiality. Although she fell into this fate, some women in Berlin School films actively seek to rupture the bonds of motherhood.

The active denial of paternal responsibility would seem commonplace in contemporary cinema—even sadly documentary. But the image of a mother abandoning her children and family still shocks, and it can be manipulated to create social pressure to conform to traditional roles. Such was the case with the Rabenmutter (raven mother) debates of the 2000s, which pitted East German traditions of collective child care and working mothers against a declining birthrate and Western individualism and conservatism.[4] This image of maternal abandonment can also serve as a metaphor for rupture with a socially prescribed role. Ulrich Köhler's second feature film, *Montag kommen die Fenster* (*Windows on Monday*, 2006), presents Nina (Isabelle Menke); her well-meaning but flaccid husband, Frieder (Hans-Jochen Wagner); and their young daughter, Charlotte (Amber Bongard). They are in the midst of a home renovation, but for Nina, the banality of their life cannot be repaired by a new coat of paint and better windows. Though married and a mother, she is utterly alone and at a loss to understand why. One day, when she is supposed to pick up her daughter, Nina disappears. She visits her brother but finds no solace there. She wanders into a Kubrickesque mountain resort hotel and walks somnambulantly through the halls. Her interactions with the guests, sexual and otherwise, are fleeting and always tinged with menace. In *her* "Overlook Hotel," she is both unsettled spirit and dangerous guest. Ultimately, she returns home, but the renovations, both to Nina and to the house, are incomplete. We understand that, with the windows not yet installed and her soul still unsettled, there is still a chance she may flee. Frieder continues the study of soft, aimless men that Köhler began in his debut, *Bungalow* (2002). Though admirable in many ways (devoted father, homebody), Frieder is unable to meld with his more liberated partner. At the time the film ends, neither he nor Nina has the tools they need to get the job done.

The central figure in a cycle of mothers portrayed in Maria Speth's searing second film, *Madonnen* (*Madonnas*, 2007), is unshakably convinced of her own righteousness. Rita (Sandra Hüller) is the single mother of five children, several of mixed race and clearly not all of the same father. When we meet her, she is screaming at her own mother on the phone. On the run, with her youngest son, J.T., strapped to her chest, she is on a quest to meet her absent father, a Belgian who has a bourgeois life with a new family. She finds him and attempts to infiltrate their domestic sphere but destroys any hope of becoming part of it when she allows her newly discovered younger half-brother to nurse from her breast as she feeds his infant nephew. Her own mother, whom she claims never mothered her, has been raising Rita's four older children. Resolute in her right to have her children together with her, Rita spirits them away to a small apartment rented with money from exes and social services. She cruises the American G.I. bars and attracts the oafish Marc, a soldier whose sweetly pathetic attempts to care for her are met with disdain. She keeps him around only as long as she needs to, exploding with rage when he oversteps his authority or questions her mothering. At a certain point, her oldest daughter asks her why she keeps making children, highlighting her obvious inability to nurture them. But having children is the one thing Rita knows she is good at. Her progeny belong to her, and of that she is fiercely proud and protective. Will she learn to care for them or shun the responsibility? At the end of Speth's film, Rita walks away.

INTERCOURSE

At the core of the Berlin School films is communicative intercourse, and much carefully structured time is spent engaging in it. Extended conversation is a critical method, as are emotive gestures and glances. But sex is also a prominent means of communication, if not always successful or particularly "sexy" in traditional cinematic terms. Male-instigated sex tends to be inept and of only marginal interest to the instigator himself. This complements the frequent portrayals of disaffected or disillusioned men, as well as the previously mentioned soft males. The most compelling sex-driven narratives are initiated by the women. One could say that the Berlin School has embraced a feminization of sex or, conversely, an emasculation of sex.

Perhaps the starkest example of the shift between old attitudes and new in the Berlin School films is the reevaluation of sex between heterosexual partners. Take the story of Gitti and Chris (Birgit Minichmayr and Lars Eidinger) in Maren Ade's *Alle Anderen* (*Everyone Else*, 2009). A young couple, vacationing at his parents' home in the warm Sardinian sun, they are thoroughly contemporary Germans. She is confident, headstrong, and amorous. He is thoughtful, sensitive, and sweetly sexy. Her opening gesture is to teach his visiting niece how to express her hatred for someone, his is to create an even more adorable stand-in/sidekick for himself out of raw ginger (which they name Schnappi). Their mutual attraction and compatibility is clear, but they are not immune to each other's potential for cruelty.

Gitti's power is located in her command of their intimacy, in response to Chris's rather demure sense of self. Gitti plays the macho during sex, pleading with Chris to leave the condom off because "it feels so

Ulrich Köhler. *Montag kommen die Fenster* (*Windows on Monday*). 2006. 35mm film, color, 88 minutes. Ilie Nastase and Isabelle Menke

Maren Ade. *Alle Anderen (Everyone Else)*. 2009. 35mm film, color, 119 minutes. Birgit Minichmayr and Lars Eidinger

much better." But he knows that would be irresponsible and slips on the safety barrier. Gitti emasculates him through her adoration, whether by feminizing him with makeup during an intimate encounter or later by defending him to Hans, a dominant male colleague. "That's how you like me," Chris observes to Gitti, "as a girl." "Yes . . . it suits you somehow," she says. Sheepishly, he asks, "Do you think I'm masculine?" She guffaws, adds a false "yes," and then tries to retract the dagger: "I'm laughing at the question." But he already knows the answer. "I'd always thought it would come naturally with age, but nothing's happening." Except for losing his hair, he lacks the traditional male markers to prove his manhood. He is liberated and lost.

Their potential downfall originates when Gitti challenges Chris to do something "masculine." He has only clichéd, antiquated indicators of what that might be. Should he focus more on career success? Perhaps he should adopt a more macho indifference toward Gitti's expressed vulnerabilities? Or is it something as banal as displays of physical prowess, like hiking up a mountain as fast as he can? Hans, who is also vacationing on the island (with his passive, pretty, and pregnant wife, Sana—Gitti's foil), becomes his false idol. A braggart and a brute, Hans is an archaic but perhaps more successful embodiment of masculinity. In response, Chris feigns more traditional masculine behavior but is ridiculously bad at it. "A terrible actor," complains Gitti. She, in turn, after digesting the implications of being labeled a ball-busting "Brunhilde" by Hans (a Wagnerian slap of the highest old-German order), attempts to become more like Sana. But— empowered and exasperated—Gitti is viscerally allergic to the charade. After a farcical, humiliating dinner party, she is first to realize that the gig is up. She cannot be Sana; she cannot tolerate Chris-as-Hans; she cannot be subservient and subdued in the presence of her dominant man. In a final desperate act to reconnect, they have passionate, unprotected sex in the garden. But even that is futile. Ultimately, the only solution is to start anew, to die and be resurrected through tenderness and the mutual acceptance of his femininity and her masculinity.

THE LABORATORY

The prominence of the female protagonist has remained a constant and critical element in the laboratory of post-Wall German identity proposed by the Berlin School films. Whether she is the young woman staring down entreaties from a lover who would mire her in a stagnant relationship or a mother who rejects traditional maternal responsibility, she offers aspects of liberation and choice that inspire forward movement. Yet there are also corrosive elements of nostalgia and greed—personified by a grieving, ghostlike mother and a would-be venture capitalist—that could subvert any real progress. These primary characters, both stimulating and cautionary, are not exclusively feminist in the traditional sense, for they provide role models for both men and women. They suggest that the most interesting new formulas for living may be derived by discarding an outdated masculine rigidity and embracing a more feminine variability. If a unified Germany is a laboratory for identity, the Berlin School directors are its researchers— their films are test tubes for experimentation, and the women who propel the narratives are the catalysts. And so I suppose my Berlinale colleague had a point: the new Germany might as well have a woman chemist from the former East trying to lead the way.

Notes

1 Marco Abel, "Imaging Germany: The (Political) Cinema of Christian Petzold," in *The Collapse of the Conventional: German Film and Its Politics at the Turn of the Twenty-first Century*, ed. Jaimey Fisher and Brad Prager (Detroit: Wayne State University Press, 2010), p. 275.
2 Petzold, quoted in Dennis Lim, "A German Wave, Focused on Today," *New York Times*, May 10, 2009, Arts and Leisure, p. 16.
3 Petzold, quoted in Nick Hasted, "In the Shadow of the Wall," *Sight & Sound* 22, no. 10 (October 2012): 51.
4 Heike Haarhoff, "Germany's Popular 'Rabenmutter,'" *German Times*, May 2007, http://www.german-times.com/index.php?option=com_content&task=view&id=367&Itemid=50.

Christian Petzold. *Jerichow*. 2008. 35mm film, color, 93 minutes. Production still. Nina Hoss

No Solutions, Only Questions:
An Encounter with Nina Hoss

Rainer Rother

The actress Nina Hoss, the face of the Berlin School, became a German film star through her collaboration with Christian Petzold. The two have made five films together, in the process creating an iconic screen type that has become further developed in each film: the lone woman warrior with a secret, one who doesn't look back, but goes her own way with determination and rigorously pursues her goal—revenge, crime, or escape. She always stands erect, looking straight ahead, perfectly poised. Only slight changes—a twitch at the corner of her mouth, a shadow across her face, an almost imperceptible gesture— betray the fact that these women's lives have gone off course.

"The Berlin School": What is that, from the point of view of its most famous actress?

The aesthetics, if anything. Who claims to be part of the Berlin School? Christian certainly doesn't. Neither does Thomas Arslan. I don't see any collective, there's no manifesto. They resemble each other in what they choose to relate—their aim is similar, one could presumably say that. You sense that there's a spiritual relationship with respect to cinema between Christian Petzold, Thomas Arslan, and Angela Schanelec. This also has to do with a

certain realism, with narratives about people living in this country. But with a distanced gaze: no solutions are presented, mostly only questions. Generally, the stories are about people who are trying to get their lives under control. To regain control.

In Christian Petzold's film Toter Mann *(Something to Remind Me, 2001), you play a phantom-like lone warrior for the first time: a young woman who wants to take revenge on her sister's killer and, to that end, worms her way into the life of an attorney. A specter of grief who wants to gain control through revenge. A sister of Petzold's earlier film characters.*

I had seen *Die innere Sicherheit* (*The State I Am In*, 2000). Its subject interested me: leftist terrorists who have lived underground for years, clinging to a radical world view while the rest of the world passes them by, continuing to change, whether for better or worse. Also, its perspective: the film is presented from the point of view of the daughter, who suffers from being on the run because she can never feel at home. Because I was more strongly rooted in the theater then and not yet so much in the "film industry," I saw it not so much as a whole new kind of cinema but simply as a terrific film.

Later I saw his earlier films *Pilotinnen* (*Pilots*, 1995), *Cuba Libre* (1996), and *Die Beischlafdiebin* (1998)—in them, there were already such women who survive. I liked them, but *Die innere Sicherheit* was still the most important one for me. I was struck by what was left out, by the way he doesn't tell everything, doesn't explain everything. That coupled with the thriller-like aspect, that fascinated me. Especially the way he employs women as protagonists—Julia Hummer as the adolescent daughter, Barbara Auer as the mother with a terrorist past—and the way he presents the family dynamic, that interested me.

The actress, the camera, the back.

What was different with Christian Petzold was that suddenly you talked about the position of the camera, why it is placed there, and why he doesn't go for a close-up but wants to see specific things played with your back to the camera, for example. That the camera's position is also the position of the narrator. And that as an actress I am able to—have to—place myself in relation to that position. Suddenly I was seeing how films are made. I began to see them differently.

For Christian Petzold, watching other films plays a mayor role in his preparation. Which ones were they for Barbara *(2012), in which you play a woman from East Germany (your third time doing this for Petzold), who wants to escape from the DDR?*

We watched Howard Hawks's *To Have and Have Not* (1944), also *Stromboli* (Roberto Rossellini, 1950)—as we did for all the other Petzold films, and which I already know by heart—and most important, *Klute* (Alan J. Pakula, 1971). Sometimes examples provide you with more as an actor than explanations or words. And Christian chooses the right scenes to communicate what he wants. In Howard Hawks, it was the first meeting between Humphrey Bogart and Lauren Bacall: both of them want a smoke, but she doesn't have any matches. He tosses a packet over to her, and she catches it. It's already clear that he's impressed, they're equals, they'll get on with each other. That relates to the characters in our film. They meet on the same level: two doctors in the DDR, fascinated by their profession, chained to it. That's their passion. Both are intelligent and sharp. And they can hold their own. She constantly challenges him, but he can take it— that's their way of flirting, just like Bogart and Bacall.

What was important in *Klute* is the way you can communicate the greatest intimacy with a single little gesture. Donald Sutherland walks through a market with Jane Fonda, buying food. The way he reaches for a melon, negotiates the price, how many tomatoes he chooses—while she stands by and watches, entranced, saying to herself, here's a person who has a grip on his life and can say: "Now you just relax, I'll take care of this." It creates a moment in which this woman can take a deep breath. You're watching this scene as she walks behind him, and then she hooks a finger into his pants pocket—that's the greatest gesture of tenderness. Christian wanted to give us that along the way.

The directors of the Berlin School tend to work with restrained emotion, with deliberate reduction. An unfamiliar area of experimentation for actors. Nonetheless, it is feelings that create expression.

Experimenting can mean various things. And with Christian Petzold, I can certainly try out different things. That's part of the special dynamic in this collaboration. There is a frame I have to work within, because I know precisely how the director conceives of the story, the objects, the characters. I know how the character is being viewed. With Christian you're fully informed about the content—I know in *Barbara* what kind of people we're presenting and just what kind of social space they move in. Just as Michael Haneke's *Das weisse Band* (*The White Ribbon*, 2009) tells me a lot about why Hitler would later become possible in Germany. In *Barbara*, viewers from the West had the sense that only now were they getting to know about the DDR. And among those from the East, there was a sense of gratitude: "Thank you for finally showing it this way." Within this framework I can try out things for myself— for example, play the contradiction between what the character is actually thinking and what she says. And the effect this perpetual balancing act has on my whole personality.

It's not a matter of squeezing more out of the tube, so to speak, of showing what a mad crying fit I can produce. I find it more interesting, actually, to depict the moment before a person cries. If somebody is already crying, I can only watch and possibly sympathize—but I'm not involved. But if I see someone struggling not to cry, that moves me a lot. Such moments are important. Then you can feel a relationship with the character, only then is it cinema. You shouldn't try to avoid any kind of identification with the character. Sometimes you can certainly go further—you see that in the "New Hollywood" films starting in the late 1960s. A lot is going on emotionally in those films, with intelligence and risk, with daring. Simply: one hands over control. Nevertheless, it's

Christian Petzold. *Barbara.* 2012. 35mm film, color, 105 minutes. Production still. Nina Hoss and Ronald Zehrfeld

Christian Petzold. *Yella.* 2007. 35mm film, color, 89 minutes. Production still. Left to right: Hans Fromm, Matthias Kapinos, and Nina Hoss

directed—it isn't true that John Cassavetes had his actors make fools of themselves for him, it's perfectly clear what they're aiming for. They're very courageous in that. I can always feel a connection to Gena Rowlands, even though as a viewer I don't understand her: I always have a feeling for where the character's attitudes are coming from. The frustration or the ease, the spirituality—the whole person, with all her contradictions. That that is allowed, that would interest me as an actress, and that is perhaps the risk involved in conceiving of something not only from the narrator's point of view.

Thomas Arslan, the Western, and Nina Hoss in the saddle.

Making *Gold* (2013) with Thomas Arslan was fun, of course, because we Germans grew up with American films, and North America was a place we yearned for. Naturally, there's something about moving around in the freedom of that landscape where the rules, the laws were being rewritten. You have the feeling that you can reinvent yourself there, that everything is possible.

  And, of course, action wasn't the main focus. In fact, the view is quite sober. I had to make do with that, that's the director's right. In a classic Western, we would have ridden fast some of the time,

which would have been fun for me. When I watch *Gold*, I find it more of a road movie than a Western. It's about city people. These people aren't made for this wilderness, aren't prepared to trek nine hundred miles through forests without trails, without maps. I found that an interesting theme: what is it that makes these people keep going? To persist in the hope that something will come. You wonder what makes people continue even when there's really no hope any longer.

In Gold, *you play a German woman in North America looking for a new beginning. What drives her onward?*

I internalized the implied back story and spun it further. The heroine, the former housemaid Emily Meyer, makes a few key statements, including, "I have a marriage behind me that wasn't so great but now doesn't seem so bad." That tells me a lot about her attitude toward life. She has tried something, but she doesn't grieve over it; she searches for something new. Even the fact that this woman has traveled alone from Bremen to New York tells me something. She isn't easily cowed. And then, for me, she's a person for whom there's no going back. There's no family waiting for her, no home. Whether she ultimately does well or not,

it's all the same, what matters is that she keeps going. Even if she loses everything at the end, she carries on alone. Something will turn up.

The films of the Berlin School follow their characters instead of telling their stories. Even so, one comes to know Emily Meyer on her ride through the Canadian forests—one feels close to her.

Because there's so much that isn't provided, I have to make the character comprehensible to myself so that I can draw on that in my acting. In *Gold*, Emily Meyer comes into a train station and has to pay for her journey. Later she says, "I earned a dollar a day." You know that it really hurts her to part with that money. So I have to play the moment in which this background is revealed. I could also have left that out, simply handed over the money, but the background story leads me to search for richness in little things. For a richness of feeling, for substance—or the hesitation, because it's so hard to give up the money. For it's also a loss of freedom.

Nobody tells me that it's a surrender, that isn't scripted anywhere. What interests me in acting is making this inner conflict visible. That is why I find omissions important: because

they give me the chance to drop a lot of little clues along the way. As a viewer, I'm also interested in discovering something about a character for myself, not having everything explained to me. The explanation might entertain me, but I don't learn anything more profound from it about these people or about life.

The View from Here

Valeska Grisebach

What does filmmaking involve? As with every other art form or activity that seeks to show or express something, filmmaking is always about something quite simple, timeless: being personal, establishing contact, discovering what one has to say, as an individual, as a group, as somebody who comes from a certain background. Telling a story, creating a mood, making a statement, or whatever, in a specific context.

. . .

My experience at film school, which continues to this day in my contact with students, is that the film world is full of rules: that's just how it is. This is what you do when you make a film. So even your own head is fully conditioned to begin with. But it only ended up being good and exciting once it became something personal. (I don't mean this in the sense of retreating into a private world or into your personal sensibility.)

. . .

I find the terms "position" or "determining a point of view" useful here, a way of simply asking yourself: Where do we start from when we put together images and want to show them? From what sort of childhood, with what family history, from which cultural context do we start things going? And I wouldn't want to distinguish between filmmakers and the audience here, but rather see them in relation to each other. What are the things we should refer to, and want to refer to, or not? What are we familiar with and what aren't we familiar with? From what perspective do we look out at the "wide wide world"?

. . .

If you think of position as something not only private but also public, social, and historical, it's also about the country we live in, of course: Germany. A country with a very difficult, multifaceted, and unfathomable history. And I don't just mean that in abstract terms but also with respect to everyday experiences, as well as within family histories. There's a past that corresponds to the present. Everything is always present at the same time.

. . .

Naturally, part of the idea of position involves the question: What sort of content and within which political or even cinematic contexts am I communicating? Where am I located? A chosen starting point that can be international.

. . .

As far as I'm concerned, the question of position also masks a plea to choose a perspective and attitude as precisely as possible. Or at least to try to do so. To narrate at eye level.

In this context, I would like to riff briefly on two key words I think about a lot: "auteur" and "realism." Let's start with realism. Again and again, there have been times—often during periods of upheaval and new beginnings—when "realism" has emerged in cinema. In many cases, it was the sign of a crisis in meaning and identity—a search for identity. Or it appears in debut features by directors who are not sure what they really have to say. At the same time, the term "realism" has repeatedly been susceptible to communicating ideology rather than truth or reality.

…

"Realism" stands for an attempt to engage with reality in one form or another, to consider it as containing something worth being told. The perspective is irrelevant here to begin with, whether hopeful, critical, pessimistic, reserved, searching, romanticizing, alienated, and so on. . . .

An attempt to make the everyday visible, to call it into memory. Even if you don't understand it. A honing of the gaze, so to speak. For "realism" is always at the same time form—that is, a stylistic device. It is a means of producing an effect. Fiction.

…

To me, realism also has to do with the documentary potential of the medium of film. The bag of tricks, the strange nature of visual spectacle. As though the materiality of film were lurking behind the origin of all filmmaking in a very concrete manner. Film material as constituting something that can record and reflect reality. (Magic!) As a medium that holds on to a moment, coincidence: a certain light, a person, people, gestures. This sensory aspect is inherent in the film's materiality, a gift. A moment of a sensual loss of control. Perhaps something is occurring that cannot be invented, just as it's (still) impossible to fabricate a human body.

…

Moreover, the "documentary moment," or realism in terms of a reflection of reality, is a window on the world, like traveling. Whether far away or around the corner. Even in many films that perhaps never intended it.

…

Now to the second key word: "auteur." I believe in auteur cinema. I believe in the author, whether as an individual, a group, or a mysterious sum of processes, of decisions. Even the many films that are not labeled auteur cinema or do not have a credited author surely contain one (or the other way round). I believe it makes sense to say that someone is speaking to me personally. By that, I don't mean to say that the author is an individual genius (divine) or some sort of natural spring from which talent flows forth. What I mean is the image of the individual, of thinking in a social context, representing the idea of relating to each other. Connecting with the history of thought and feeling, social discourse and criticism.

What does that mean for filmmaking in concrete terms? What does that mean for the rules of filmmaking? I also believe it's relevant to think about that with respect to our current situation: what was the social or political backdrop that made us settle upon pure entertainment, on "industry," in Germany, and when did an auteur movement arise? To what extent, for example, has reunification changed the concept of authorship? What does our present situation look like? What context of public objectives and political discourse do I find myself in as an author?

…

This all seems to me like a small step in the right direction, toward a connection between personal identity and internationalism. Where do I come from? This doesn't mean denying your own identity. But it's also about being interested in something else, entering into a relationship with others. Getting out of the provinces. It would be nice if these films could communicate and be seen beyond our own country's borders. And to complement this, it would be nice to have an audience, a section of the public that takes an interest in the diversity and variety of cinema.

Film—perhaps due to its economic potential—appears to be especially susceptible to accusations of ideology. But I simply don't believe that this is the case. I think of film as a very open, free medium. There is somehow something quite stimulating, vital, and comforting in the fact that there is no one proper direction. Cinema is experience, context, narrative, but always uncharted territory too, a place for experimentation. The more confusion and the less ideology, the better.

…

Excerpts from a talk at the film symposium "Filmavantgarde und Kunst: Innovative Antworten auf neue kulturelle und technologische Herausforderungen" ("Avant-garde Film and Art: Innovative Responses to New Cultural and Technological Challenges"), Nordrhein Westfalen, 2006. Originally published, in German, in Valeska Grisebach, "Von hier aus," Revolver 16 (May 2007): 74–93.

On the Move:
Thomas Arslan's
Kinetic Cinema

Katja Nicodemus

Thomas Arslan. *Gold*. 2013. Digital video, color, 101 minutes. Nina Hoss

Between 1830 and 1900, millions of Germans trapped in bitter poverty sought their fortunes abroad and emigrated to North America. But it was only with Thomas Arslan's Western, *Gold* (2013), that this astonishing fact became a part of German cinema. A German Western? From the Berlin School? A Western produced out of a film movement known for investigating contemporary feelings about life and generational issues? And known, too, for a calm camera gaze that hardly seems appropriate to American landscapes and pioneer myths?

My meeting with Thomas Arslan took place in Kreuzberg, the Berlin district with the highest proportion of Turkish residents. Arslan has lived here for many years. And somehow it seems especially right to be in this neighborhood, surrounded by Turkish cafés, Turkish vegetable sellers, and the Adana Grill, talking about shifting perspectives on immigration. "Today, Germany sees itself burdened by immigration," Arslan says. "But the country once produced a huge number of immigrants itself. There was a major exodus, a huge movement. Only it doesn't fit so nicely into the pattern of our history books."

Thomas Arslan appears reticent yet expectant. In his Western he would have been the close-lipped horseman packing the saddlebags rather than the big-talking ringleader. While rummaging through photo albums in an antiquarian bookstore, he came upon some historical photographs of German pioneers and gold seekers. "These pictures wouldn't let me go," he says, "the faces, these old photos of Germans who had nothing and nothing to lose." He began doing research, reading diaries and digging into an almost-forgotten chapter of German history. In *Gold*, Nina Hoss plays the former housemaid Emily Meyer, a woman who, toward the end of the nineteenth century, makes her way with a small group of émigrés through more than nine hundred miles of Canadian wilderness to Dawson and the mouth of the Klondike. It is a dangerous trek.

For Arslan, the challenge was not to glorify the landscape but to expose its hostility. The cameraman, Patrick Orth, again and again presents shots in which it looks as though the landscape itself is watching the

foreigners making their way through undergrowth, along rivers, over hills and mountainsides. "Because they don't really make progress, the panoramic expanse that first held out promise turns into the opposite," Arslan says. "It becomes claustrophobic." Despite the grueling trip, there is no turning back for Emily, a tall, blond embodiment of pure determination. But precisely what drives her forward and what lies behind her don't need to be told. Only through movement and through the tasks along the way does Emily invent herself as a character, in action, before our eyes. This antipsychological aspect, which preserves her autonomy, and her mystery, is perhaps the most telling Berlin School feature in this Western.

In the mid-1990s, Arslan—along with Angela Schanelec and Christian Petzold, two of his colleagues from the dffb film school in Berlin—became one of the first protagonists of this directorial movement. While Schanelec, the seismographer, observes her characters with a distanced eye as their lives gradually fall apart, and while Petzold creates dense spaces in which the melodramas that are taking place can always be interpreted politically, Arslan is the great companion—the director at eye level. In his work, the cinematographic form always appears to derive from the individual moment, to accompany the characters like an accomplice and to ally itself with them.

And, of course, the genre film—with its predictable characteristics and stereotypes—has always been an ally of its heroes and heroines. Arslan says that, for him as a director, it was a boon to be able to rely on the preexisting pattern of the Western: "The challenging part is making the pattern strike a responsive chord in one's own way." It is Arslan's long takes, capturing even the smallest detail, that create the space in which this chord can resonate. In this space the Western is reduced to its practical, everyday essence: the drudgery of packing saddles and putting up tents; the falls, accidents, and injuries; the search for the right route. His film requires no outside enemies, no external action, because the

real enemy is the trail itself. By concentrating on movement, Arslan gives the genre a rigor and an inner tension, using "antiaction" to expose the internal experience of being a pioneer.

In his first excursion into genre, his film *Im Schatten* (*In the Shadows*, 2010), Arslan was already interested in his characters' activities and movements—this time through the space of the city of Berlin. The untouristy gaze that directors of the Berlin School have always cast on the German capital leads here into inhospitable, down-at-the-heels areas. Arslan's main character, Trojan (Mišel Matičević), just released from prison, lives in seedy hotel rooms, meets with accomplices in back courtyards and parking lots at the edges of shopping malls, searches out a fence in a construction shed. Arslan breaks the heist movie down into a series of precisely observed actions, often filmed in real time. Counting bills, taking weapons apart and putting them back together, committing the crime itself, the rattling of the getaway car, the drive to the hideout. His constant focus is on the planning, preparation, and execution of a crime, the crass and intricate mechanics of it. One could describe the result as a suspenseful expedition into everyday criminality. Or as a thriller in the tradition of Jean-Pierre Melville, but without that filmmaker's heightened reality.

The assurance with which Arslan employs the patterns of the crime genre derived mainly from focusing his filmic gaze on his own environment. The son of a German clerk and a Turkish construction engineer, he was born in Braunschweig in 1962, attended grammar school in Istanbul, and subsequently moved with his parents to Berlin. In the mid-1990s, Arslan's Berlin School films intersected with another trend in German cinema: a German-Turkish cinema suddenly came to the screen, with subject matter that was no longer limited to the integration difficulties of first-generation parents. The balancing act between tradition, family, and big-city socialization was still there, to be sure, but it was thrust into the background. "The Algerian French needed thirty years to develop their *cinéma beur*. We are quicker. We're already getting started."[1] So the director Fatih Akin proclaimed in 1998, when his feature-film debut, *kurz und schmerzlos* (*Short Sharp Shock*), came out—a buddy movie set in the multicultural milieu of petty gangsters in Hamburg-Altona. When Akin's wild love story *Gegen die Wand* (*Head-On*, 2004) won the Berlinale prize, this cinema celebrated its international breakthrough.

At almost the same time that Akin was making his directorial debut, Thomas Arslan made *Geschwister* (*Brothers and Sisters*, 1997), the first film to focus on the world of German-Turkish youth from their own perspective. His camera always stays a step back, giving the siblings Erol (Tamer Yiğit), Ahmed (Savaş Yurderi), and Leyla (Serpil Turhan) a framework within which to play out the conflicts in their lives. Clichés like the collisions between worlds are irrelevant to him, Arslan claimed, in a conversation about *Geschwister* that we had in 1997—in fact, in the same Berlin-Kreuzberg café.[2] He was more interested in mental states. For example, the adolescent in-betweenness of the two dissimilar brothers Erol and Ahmed. One lives day to day and, with no prospects, considers going back to Turkey to do his military service. The other, by contrast, speaks perfect German, is at the top of his class, and has a girlfriend. On their forays through Berlin-Kreuzberg, the brothers talk about everything: love and money problems, family and future worries, the coolest names for pit bulls. Their walks through the neighborhood become the expression of a drifting approach to life that can no longer be identified as German, Turkish, or German-Turkish.

Thomas Arslan. *Geschwister*. 1997. Left to right: Mohamed Khalil, Bülent Akil, Tamer Yiğit, Savaş Yurderi, Bilge Bingül

Thomas Arslan. *Dealer*. 1999. 35mm film, color, 74 minutes. Tamer Yiğit

There is nothing in German cinema to compare with the way Arslan makes events on Berlin's neighborhood streets into a film world and a universal formula for youth. One has to look to France instead. The long takes and the close collaboration with adolescents is reminiscent of Jacques Doillon; the development of a style out of the process of shooting recalls Maurice Pialat; the passion for original sound, Jean-Marie Straub and Danièle Huillet. Arslan admits to having been influenced by a certain kind of French cinema, but in the truest sense he has no style of his own. He says this with his characteristic reticence, which becomes even greater the more one tries to pin him down. He assures me that he doesn't make programmatic decisions. "A lot develops unconsciously or half-consciously, nothing systematically." He speaks of predilections, biases, tendencies. "The form always develops from the material."

In *Dealer* (1999) and *Der schöne Tag* (*A Fine Day*, 2001)—the second and third parts of his trilogy —Arslan remains at eye level with his German-Turkish protagonists, in that he develops a special cinematographic form for each of them. *Dealer* is about a young father and drug dealer (Tamer Yiğit) who wanders through his own life and the city as though lost. Even though Arslan once again casts a virtually documentary eye on the everyday business of dealing—standing around, waiting, sizing up—this time, the helplessness and the disorientation of the young criminal, Can, are set off against stylized tableaus. "I wanted strong light, intense, 'pretty' colors, precisely to show that Can, owing to his inability to give direction to his life, finds no access to what one could call happiness or beauty," Arslan says. In *Der schöne Tag* he follows a budding actress on her paths through Berlin, from casting to a café, to her mother's place, to a flirtatious date. Arslan's naturalistic handling of light and a story that also comprises randomly narrated situations combine with the excursions of the lead actress (Serpil Turhan) to produce a summery, airy state of ambiguity .

That Arslan's cinema derives directly from the theme and the material is illustrated by a film that at first and possibly even second viewing does not fit into his oeuvre, but accords very well with the thematic and generational swings of Berlin School films. This is *Ferien* (*Vacation*, 2007), a piece of intimate theater set outdoors. It focuses on the attitude toward life of a West Berlin–educated bourgeoisie that has to recognize that its world, once enclosed and ultimately protected by the Wall, has begun to collapse more than it originally anticipated.

A Berlin family gathers at the parents' country house for a summer holiday. Surprises crop up, old resentments are triggered anew, some lives will drift apart but others cling together, full of hope. At the beginning, the actresses Karoline Eichhorn and Angela Winkler are seated at a small garden table. The mother earnestly asks her daughter how she is doing. The daughter responds a bit irritably but with shattering candor. She talks about reorienting herself, about her translation work, which doesn't give her enough income. And suddenly two generational attitudes pervade the picture: on the one hand, that of a smug bourgeois class, now retired and saturated in self-assurance; on the other, its more or less washed-up children, who no longer have the means and perhaps also no longer the self-confidence to live according to their parents' standards.

In *Ferien*, Arslan's characters are not in motion for once. The space of the film consists of a house and garden that the camera treats like a stage. Entrances and exits, ensemble scenes and silent intervals become a roundelay in which the members of the family appear to coexist rather than forming a unit. Meanwhile—between the rustling of leaves and chirping of crickets, the small errands and additional arrivals—the film raises familiar questions that are perpetually being posed in new ways: Should a couple separate because of an affair, or not? How does a person reinvent his life at age sixty? And why does one always quarrel with one's parents and siblings in the same old way?

Two genre films, Berlin neighborhood walks, a family history. Western pioneers, criminals, German-Turkish youth, the educated bourgeoisie. These characters do not tell us their stories, they themselves are the story. When we become involved in their movement, they disclose their separate worlds to us. If we follow them further, we get beyond what we thought we already knew. Like his kindred spirits of the Berlin School, Thomas Arslan, observer of movement, moves through a new German cinema.

Notes

The interview with Thomas Arslan took place in Berlin on January 20, 2013.

1 Fatih Akin, quoted in Anke Leweke, "Der neue deutsche Film ist da!" *Tip Berlin*, no. 22 (1998): 19.
2 Katja Nicodemus, "Cruising Kreuzberg," *Tip Berlin*, no. 25 (1997): 42.

Thomas Arslan. *Ferien* (*Vacation*). 2007. 35mm film, color, 91 minutes. Angela Winkler

I came to filmmaking by watching films. For a long time, watching films was occasionally a pleasant solitary experience, but no more important than reading comics, listening to music, or playing soccer.

In Essen, where I spent most of my youth, there was a theater called Lux am Stern. When I was about ten, a not-inconsiderable part of the excitement of going to a movie there was getting into films approved for only twelve- or even seventeen-year-olds and up. Ultimately more memorable than what these films left me with was the theater itself. From the outside, it was an unspectacular flat-roofed structure right at an intersection in Essen-Rüttenscheid. The auditorium of the Lux am Stern was huge, bigger than one would have guessed from the outside. Through all the years I saw films there, the auditorium had a crack in the ceiling. A crack that ran down the center of the entire ceiling. Since I attended only matinees at that point, during the screening it was possible to see daylight filtering into the dark hall through this narrow crack. Instead of destroying the illusion, this pale slit of light on the ceiling made going to a movie even more unreal for me than it would have been otherwise. It made the darkness even darker, the isolation of the space even more isolated, and what was taking place on the screen even stranger. The Lux am Stern, long since torn down, was always for me the city's nicest cinema.

The Cinema of Life

Thomas Arslan

A few years later I was given a reflex camera, and I soon became passionately interested in photography. At that time I first attended a presentation by the film club at Essen's adult education center. I ended up there more or less by accident—it wasn't as if I was driven by a passion for film. That theater was anything but a temple to film. An ugly multipurpose space, neutral at best, in which the Essen filmmaker Werner Biedermann screened selected films twice a week. Rarely were there more than ten people in the audience. Often there were fewer. There he showed films by Rossellini, Bresson, Godard, and Eustache. The films I saw there caught me wholly unprepared. They opened a floodgate. Without knowing what I was looking for, I had found something that has never let me go.

Even before I finished high school I knew I wanted to be a filmmaker. In 1983 I saw À nos amours (To Our Loves), by Maurice Pialat, during the film festival in Berlin. The film, which was screened in the competition but attracted little attention, left me distraught. At the time, I thought of myself as someone with a certain knowledge of cinema. À nos amours completely swept away that pedantic certainty.

In one of the finest moments of the film, the young Sandrine Bonnaire returns home from her boyfriend late one night. She tries to enter her parents' apartment as silently as possible. In a long shot you see her father, played by Maurice Pialat himself, turn off the television at the edge of the picture and quickly put on a work smock. Having noticed her arrival, he goes over to a table with tailoring paraphernalia,

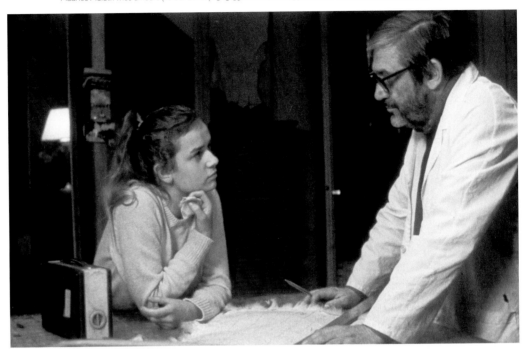

where he pretends to be busy. When they meet in the living room, the two at first assume their familiar roles. She, the good, still-childlike daughter. He, the hardworking father concerned for the welfare of his child. He subjects her to a brief grilling about why she is coming home so late. She replies evasively. But both soon tire of their roles. An intimate, personal conversation develops (clearly something rare for them). The camera has moved in very close to their faces. They are now two people talking to each other, first of all, and no longer father and daughter. Finally, the father, who has taken off his smock again, tells her that he is going to abandon the family because he wants to live with another woman. The greatest intimacy the two have ever had comes at the moment of their parting. The camera then moves back into a medium shot. The daily routine returns in the way they say good night to each other. They resume their familiar roles. It is moving to see how Pialat and Bonnaire play out the transition from one to the other. And how the camera responds.

The narrative of *À nos amours* is so digressive that it defies all the criteria of elegance. The omissions are not ellipses the viewer has to fill in a way calculated by the filmmaker. They correspond to the vexing fissures in the self and in those close to you. The film also respects its characters to such a degree that it doesn't claim to know anything about these dark regions.

In *À nos amours*, elaborately planned sequences alternate with simple shot-countershot scenes (scorned by cineastes). The transparent performances of the actors, the decisions about when the camera should be close to them or at a distance—in Pialat, all this is based more on a dramaturgy of life than on that of the cinema. This seemingly artless film struck me like a bolt of lightning and quite literally showed me that the cinema knows no rules.

This statement was originally published, in German, in Thomas Arslan, "Kinoerfahrungen," *Revolver* 13 (December 2005): 92–101.

Moving On:
The Next New Wave

Dennis Lim

Opposite and below: Benjamin Heisenberg. *Der Räuber* (*The Robber*). 2010. 35mm film, color, 90 minutes. Production stills. Andreas Lust

It is a testament to the vigor of the Berlin School that the movement, now well into its second decade, can be said to have spawned a subsequent generation. But it is also a credit to the individual films pulled into its orbit that this label, a contrivance to begin with, has long ceased to be accurate or even very useful. As first defined, the Berlin School referred principally to Thomas Arslan, Christian Petzold, and Angela Schanelec—three graduates of the prestigious dffb, or Deutsche Film- und Fernsehakademie Berlin (the German Film and Television Academy), who began their careers in the 1990s. Most filmmakers from the next generation, several of whom launched their careers with their graduation films, have no direct association with the dffb or with Berlin, although most are now based in the city.[1] This generation emerged in the wake of Petzold's *Die innere Sicherheit* (*The State I Am In*, 2000), at that point the most commercially successful of the Berlin School films, with a cluster of auspicious debut features arriving early last decade: Valeska Grisebach's *Mein Stern* (*Be My Star*, 2001), Ulrich Köhler's *Bungalow* (2002), Henner Winckler's *Klassenfahrt* (*School Trip*, 2002), and Christoph Hochhäusler's *Milchwald* (*This Very Moment*, 2003), among others.

The media-friendly idea of a new wave has helped raise the profile of many deserving filmmakers, but it has also become a more elastic, not to mention reductive, concept now that most of them have two or three features to their name. It has also served to rope in some filmmakers—like Maren Ade, Maria Speth, and the South African–born, dffb-educated Pia Marais—whose work is only tangentially related. But even though the notion of an all-encompassing Berlin School obscures the individuality of its supposed members, it is hardly spurious to suggest that a collective of like-minded voices exists in contemporary German independent cinema.

No group manifesto has materialized, but there is plenty of cross-pollination. The indispensable cinematographer Reinhold Vorschneider has worked with Speth, Benjamin Heisenberg, and Hochhäusler;

Heisenberg and Hochhäusler are cofounders of the long-running *Revolver* magazine. Given the number of former and part-time critics, academics, and all-around cinephiles in its midst, it is no surprise that the evolution of the Berlin School—and it has evolved, in more interesting ways than most so-called movements—rests on an interplay between theory and practice, a compulsion among its affiliates both to discuss and to demonstrate what it means to make films in and about Germany today.

Berlin School films are often termed "minimalist," associated with reticent characters and long takes —an exacting house style that can be seen as a reaction to mainstream storytelling conventions and, in particular, to the glut of clumsy escapist comedies and bloated historical dramas that dominated German cinema in the 1980s. But "minimalism" is an inadequate, perhaps even misleading label—as is "realism." These films use extreme precision to achieve ambiguous, sometimes deeply strange effects. They insist on an engagement with the real world, though often through a hyperreal clarity that is itself a kind of stylization. Rooted in observation and the materiality of the world, they look intently at the everyday "until it looks back, until it becomes mysterious," as Petzold once put it.[2] They are, perhaps above all, movies that enact a way of seeing—and, as such, more political than they may first seem.

The younger generation of Berlin School filmmakers has proved especially adept at harmonizing form and content, in films that reflect their thematic concerns in subtly self-reflexive ways. The opening of Köhler's first feature, *Bungalow*, encapsulates the tension between mobility and stasis that defines many of these movies. A long panning shot follows an army convoy as it pulls off a highway and into a rest area, then accompanies the soldiers as they enter a fast-food joint. As the trucks depart, the camera comes to a halt, assuming the perspective of the one soldier who has—for reasons that will remain unclear—stayed behind. Paul (Lennie Burmeister) is an emblematic Berlin School protagonist, unmoored and apathetic. Broadly speaking, this is a cinema of drift and alienation, and in addition to the frequently cited reference point of France's so-called Second New Wave (Jean Eustache, Philippe Garrel, and perhaps most of all Maurice Pialat), it is indebted to the modernist meanderings of Michelangelo Antonioni and contemporary Asian cinema (it is not hard to detect the stray influence of Tsai Ming-liang, Wong Kar-wai, or Apichatpong Weerasethakul). But if the movies reflect an awareness of global film culture and film history, they are also determinedly local in their concerns.

The sense of place that emerges so powerfully is often of Germany as a nonplace, a phantom zone in both sociopolitical and existential senses, where the hangover of reunification persists, replete with false promises and deep insecurities. The films gravitate to liminal zones, like the German-Polish border regions in Hochhäusler's *Milchwald* and Winckler's *Klassenfahrt*, or the barely inhabited houses under renovation in *Milchwald* and in Köhler's second feature, *Montag kommen die Fenster* (*Windows on Monday*, 2006), where it is a wife and mother who goes AWOL.

Sometimes the in-between space is one that straddles reality and fantasy, as happens in Hochhäusler's work. *Milchwald*, one of the Berlin School's many depictions of fractured families, is also quite pointedly an updated fairy tale, riffing on the Grimm brothers' Hansel and Gretel. In Hochhäusler's second film, *Falscher Bekenner* (*I Am Guilty*, 2005), the teenage protagonist (Constantin von Jascheroff) confesses to crimes he has not committed—not just as a cry for attention but in a bid to create a new identity, a new reality, for

himself. He's seen on nightly visits to an autobahn rest stop where he hooks up with leather bikers, though they too may be fictions of his own imagining.

The strain of realism that defines the Berlin School is generally so intensified that it can breed disorientation, become prone to rupture and slippage: realism less as a tool of documentation than a medium of transformation. Grisebach's *Sehnsucht* (*Longing*, 2006), an anguished romantic triangle in a rural setting, unfolds in a register of quiet, sustained naturalism, but the slow-building intensity gives way to a sleight-of-hand coda that vaults the film into the realm of fable. Ade's *Der Wald vor lauter Bäumen* (*The Forest for the Trees*, 2003) has a similarly deft and devastating conclusion: a passage into the surreal that grants its long-suffering heroine (Eva Löbau), a misfit schoolteacher, a transcendent moment of release.

Observation and perception are the explicit subjects of Heisenberg's first film, *Schläfer* (*Sleeper*, 2005), in which Johannes (Bastian Trost), a German scientist, is asked by the secret service to keep tabs

on Farid (Mehdi Nebbou), a Muslim colleague suspected of involvement in a terrorist cell. The love-triangle mechanics and the topical subject matter are, to an extent, red herrings in a film whose primary interest is philosophical and whose careful distance from its characters allows us to consider how a tiny shred of information and the mere prospect of surveillance affect the observer and the observed, not to mention the viewer. (Heisenberg is the grandson of the physicist Werner Heisenberg, author of the uncertainty principle, which is commonly, if inaccurately, conflated with the observer effect, which refers to the changes that the act of observation brings about.)

From its very first scene, which plants the seed of doubt that activates the plot, *Schläfer* establishes a link between Johannes's authority as an informant and the role of the storyteller-filmmaker: "You determine what you tell us and how we see him," the agent advises him. The films of the Berlin School are intimately concerned with narrative as epistemology, with how stories explain the world, or fail to do so. It is by and large a de-dramatized cinema, suspicious of the seductions of narrative, in which decisive moments—a boy jumping off a pier in *Klassenfahrt*, a young woman falling off a balcony in *Sehnsucht*—are oddly haunting in part because we barely register them as they happen. Did we see it, or just think we did? But these are also films that believe in cinema's capacity to render the invisible visible, to make epiphanies tangible, to show the convergence of forces that bring a man to the impasse of loving two women, or turn a pretend criminal into a real one.

While the Berlin School has garnered critical support at home and abroad—especially in France, where the films inspired the critical coinage "Nouvelle Vague Allemande" (German New Wave)—it has also faced a backlash from some sectors in the German film industry. The most common accusations dismiss the films as commercially marginal and indict them as bourgeois, apolitical navel-gazing. Köhler's polemical essay "Why I Don't Make 'Political' Films" is a concise rebuttal and a counterattack on self-important prestige movies. "A cinema that doesn't want to participate in the exploitation of history is not politically ignorant," he writes, arguing for the importance—as Jean-Luc Godard did before him—of making films politically, as opposed to merely seeking out nominally political subjects.[3] Some are friendlier salvos, as in the case of Dominik Graf, the veteran genre director who has criticized the Berlin School filmmakers for their "distrust of language, of communication" and maintains that "instead of expanding narrative possibilities," their films represent "a narrowing of gaze."[4]

Most of these charges understate the variety of films under the Berlin School umbrella. Grisebach's *Sehnsucht* and Ade's *Alle Anderen* (*Everyone Else*, 2009) are radical love stories by any measure, harrowingly precise and tender diagrams of erotic desire and mortification that go some way toward reversing decades' worth of gendered conventions. And while their protagonists tend to be recessive and oblivious, Berlin School films are hardly blind to the day-to-day realities of contemporary Germany, most obviously in the work of Arslan, who has long explored cross-cultural identity, but also in Heisenberg's *Schläfer* and in Speth's provocative *Madonnen* (*Madonnas*, 2007), whose white heroine (Sandra Hüller), involved with a series of African American soldiers stationed in Germany, is the unlikely mother of a growing biracial brood.

Maria Speth. *Madonnen* (*Madonnas*). 2007. 35mm film, color, 120 minutes. Sandra Hüller with children

But the criticisms leveled at the Berlin School films are just as often self-directed. The careers of the movement's key exponents have diverged and progressed in ways that reflect a constant sense of flux, born of habitual self-examination. The more ambitious filmmakers, perhaps sensing the risk of mannerism and insularity, are pushing beyond familiar settings, looking for new geographic terrain. Köhler, in his third feature, *Schlafkrankheit* (*Sleeping Sickness*, 2011), transposes his recurring themes of home and estrangement to a larger geopolitical canvas, tracing the tangled senses of alienation that afflict two Europeans in Africa (a German doctor in Cameroon, and the French doctor of African descent sent from Paris to evaluate him). Hochhäusler's *Unter dir die Stadt* (*The City Below*, 2010), an oblique tale of boardroom and bedroom intrigue, orchestrates a zombified ritual of seduction and repulsion in what amounts to an abstract, free-floating space, the glass canyons of global capital.

Some are moving toward an embrace of genre. Arslan, of late, has moved further in this direction with the Melvillian gangster thriller *Im Schatten* (*In the Shadows*, 2010) and the neo-Western *Gold* (2013). Among the younger generation, the most committed genre exercise is Heisenberg's *Der Räuber* (*The Robber*, 2010), set in Austria and based on a true story. It features a hero defined almost exclusively by his twin obsessions: he's a marathon runner and a bank robber, driven to attain a state of perpetual motion. The result is many films in one: action thriller, love story, character study, and existential parable, not to mention a literally sped-up, endorphin-rush variation on the familiar Berlin School dialectic of movement and stasis. The project that to this day best encapsulates the movement's evolution—its willingness to evolve—is the three-part, made-for-television *Dreileben* (*Three Lives*, 2011), which had its roots in a correspondence among Petzold, Graf, and Hochhäusler first published in *Revolver*.[5] Their lively exchange, which weighed the possibilities and traps of genre cinema vs. auteur cinema and revealed both mutual concerns and sharp disagreements, compelled the filmmakers to put theory into practice. Beginning with the tabloidish

Christian Petzold. *Etwas Besseres als den Tod* (*Beats Being Dead*), from *Dreileben* (*Three Lives*). 2011. 35mm film, color, 88 minutes. Jacob Matschenz and Luna Mijović

Dominik Graf. *Komm mir nicht nach* (*Don't Follow Me Around*), from *Dreileben* (*Three Lives*). 2011. 16mm film, color, 89 minutes. Left to right: Mišel Matičević, Susanne Wolff, and Jeanette Hain

Christoph Hochhäusler. *Eine Minute Dunkel* (*A Minute of Darkness*), from *Dreileben* (*Three Lives*). 2011. Digital video, color, 90 minutes

scenario of a convicted killer and sex offender who escapes while paying his last respects to his mother in a hospital, each filmmaker found his own entry point into his own film. Petzold deals with a victim-to-be; Graf, with one of the investigators; and Hochhäusler, with the killer himself. The effect is prismatic, a central incident refracted through three contrasting perspectives: two generations of the Berlin School and a friendly adversary looking in from the outside.

Petzold's *Etwas Besseres als den Tod* (*Beats Being Dead*), an unstable hybrid of romantic tragedy and slasher noir, focuses on two young people who cross paths with the killer: Johannes (Jacob Matschenz), a premed student working as a nurse to fulfill his national-service obligations, and Ana (Luna Mijović), a chambermaid and Bosnian émigré. Like Petzold's *Yella* (2007), the film is a ghost story, set among the living dead, and as in so many of his other movies, Petzold inscribes cold, hard truths of class and money into almost every scene, fusing erotic tensions with socioeconomic ones.

Graf's *Komm mir nicht nach* (*Don't Follow Me Around*), packed with revealing tangents and glancing micro-observations, makes a virtue of skittishness. The distractable camera snoops, wanders, lingers on odd details, and the narrative likewise keeps shifting its attention. The protagonist, Jo (Jeanette Hain), is a police psychologist, called in to investigate the escaped killer. But the real point of her trip to Thuringia (the rural region in central Germany where the story unfolds) is an internal-affairs inquiry into local corruption. The core of the story, in any case, turns out to be Jo's reunion with an old friend, Vera (Susanne Wolff), an unexpected conduit to an ex-flame. Both women discover that they were once in love with the same man at the same time, unaware of each other's existence. Jo and Vera's relationship—which gets more complicated as the women compare notes while withholding information—reinforces *Dreileben*'s larger context: a world of imperfect knowledge.

In *Eine Minute Dunkel* (*A Minute of Darkness*), Hochhäusler turns back to the primary narrative, which he propels to a genre payoff and imbues with philosophical richness. A brooding dual-character study, it follows the killer (Stefan Kurt) in his interlude of freedom (overwhelmed by the natural world, rendered with tactile immediacy by Reinhold Vorschneider) and the grizzled policeman (Eberhard Kirchberg) who revisits the original case, haunted by a missing minute in the surveillance footage of the crime. This lacuna speaks to the impossibility of certainty in the absence of observable evidence, the danger of imposing stories onto what we cannot know for sure. Narrative, to quote Hochhäusler, is something that "contaminates the picture"—a lie, and what's more, a lie that could become the truth.[6]

Dreileben takes a cubist approach to storytelling, reinforcing a basic fact of human coexistence: shared experiences reverberate in different ways. With three filmmakers working in concert but also autonomously, subjectivity is built into the project. Together, the three films offer many of the pleasures of a puzzle movie: stories intersect and characters move between foreground and background; ellipses are filled in and questions answered, one segment providing a (sometimes literal) reverse angle on another. But instead of merely connecting the dots, each installment enriches and complicates the others. Taken together, these stories attest to the limits of knowledge and the potential of imaginative empathy. The self-contained modesty of each film belies the immensity of the project. A self-imposed challenge to the Berlin School that both defies its conventions and breathes new life into them, *Dreileben* conjures not just three lives but worlds of possibilities.

Notes

1 Ulrich Köhler and Henner Winckler attended the Hochschule für bildende Künste (University of Fine Arts) in Hamburg; Maren Ade, Benjamin Heisenberg, and Christoph Hochhäusler, the Hochschule für Fernsehen und Film München (the University of Television and Film Munich); Maria Speth, the Hochschule für Film und Fernsehen "Konrad Wolf" (the Film and Television University in Potsdam); and Valeska Grisebach, the Filmakademie Wien (Vienna Film Academy).
2 Petzold, in Marco Abel, "The Cinema of Identification Gets on My Nerves: An Interview with Christian Petzold," *Cineaste* 33 (Summer 2008), http://www.cineaste.com/articles/an-interview-with-christian-petzold.htm.
3 Ulrich Köhler, "Warum ich keine 'politischen' Filme mache," *New Filmkritik*, April 23, 2007, http://newfilmkritik.de/archiv/2007-04/warum-ich-keine-politischen-filme-mache; published in English as "Why I Don't Make 'Political' Films," *Cinema Scope* 38 (2009): 10–13.
4 Graf, in Dominik Graf, Christian Petzold, and Christoph Hochhäusler, "Mailwechsel Berliner Schule," *Revolver* 16 (May 2007): 12. Translation from a Berlinale handout.
5 Dominik Graf, Christian Petzold, and Christoph Hochhäusler, "Mailwechsel Berliner Schule," *Revolver* 16 (May 2007): 6–41. Excerpts published in English as *Dreileben*, http://www.berlinale.de/external/de/filmarchiv/doku_pdf/20113081.pdf.
6 Hochhäusler, ibid., p. 17. Translation from a Berlinale handout.

Benjamin Heisenberg. *Der Räuber*. 2010. Production still. Andreas Lust

Form Follows

Benjamin Heisenberg

A machine functions, as does a theory, a construct. A person who merely functions is one of the saddest things to encounter in this world. That also applies to a story. What matters is the author's personal point of view. The more individual and particular the narrative, the more universal its content.

In art school I learned that any content you want to express requires its own specific technique. You wouldn't exhibit a small pencil drawing on a large neon yellow mat, because such a background would distract from what is essential. I have the impression that cinematic methods—quite apart from their role within the narrative—have such a great effect of their own that they often function like that neon yellow mat, and the qualities of the drawing thus remain unappreciated. In the drawing, I recognize a person. In the mat, I see only the impact of a color.

The assessment "it works" shows how much the viewers' reaction has become the primary criterion. The engagement of the viewer has become the door to all the other levels of the work. In many films, this door is pushed wide open with great verve, but there's no point in going further, because there's generally a yawning emptiness behind it. People, wars, tragedies serve as spectacular MacGuffins for raging pyrotechnical effects. As David Lynch says, "Things go so fast when you're making a movie now that

Left: Still life, Nara, Japan. 2010

Center: My first real revolver, from 1845, Lucerne, Switzerland. 2009

Right: Contemporary tranquility, on a flight back to Munich from New York. 2007

you're not able to give the world enough—what it deserves. It wants to be lived in a little bit, it's got so much to offer and you're going just a little too fast. It's just sad."[1] The stories are generally perfectly imaginative and grippingly structured. The directors have studied their film history. They know every trick and keep their eye on the viewer, direct every emotion with a carrot and a stick. And yet these films are like drugs that leave me no other choice but to take them again and again. Between those rushes, there's a painful nothingness.

Alfred Hitchcock, in a conversation with François Truffaut, describes a film with the basic idea of "twenty-four hours in the life of a city." "So there's a cycle, beginning with the gleaming fresh vegetables and ending with the mess that's poured into the sewers. Thematically the cycle would show what people do to good things. Your theme might almost be the rottenness of humanity. You could take it through the whole city, look at everything, film everything, and show all of that."[2] See everything, to me that's the general requirement, then I can productively choose for myself, select the essential aspects with which to present what I have in mind. If it is only the matter of a box-office success, I will limit myself to showing only what is essential. Anything that goes beyond that doesn't pay in such calculations. Just as in figure skating, in art there's the compulsory element and the freestyle element. To sell well, it's enough to do the compulsory part well. To be better than all the rest, the freestyle part has to reveal your most personal feelings and values. Only then does a film strike people's hearts.

Notes

This statement was originally published, in German, in Benjamin Heisenberg, "Form Follows," *Revolver* 3 (June 1999): 102–7.
1 David Lynch, *Lynch on Lynch*, ed. Chris Rodley, rev. ed. (New York: Faber and Faber, 2005), p. 56.
2 Hitchcock, quoted in Francois Truffaut, *Hitchcock*, rev. ed. (New York: Simon and Schuster, 1984), p. 320.

Acknowledgments

Throughout the research and organization of the first English-language monograph and MoMA film exhibition dedicated to the Berlin School, we have been fortunate to work with generous, insightful, and enthusiastic colleagues. At The Museum of Modern Art, we first extend warm thanks to Glenn D. Lowry, Director, for his support and encouragement. We are tremendously appreciative of Marie-Josée Kravis, President, and Jerry I. Speyer, Chairman, of the Museum's Board of Trustees, for their backing of and keen interest in the Film Department. For their enduring championing of film projects and programs, we are furthermore indebted to the Film Committee, notably Committee Chair Ted Sann and Vice Chair Kenneth Kuchin, as well as former Chairs Anna Deavere Smith and James G. Niven.

Esteemed colleagues throughout the Museum have been exceedingly helpful in the successful execution of this project, particularly James Gara, Chief Operating Officer; Ramona Bronkar Bannayan, Senior Deputy Director, Exhibitions, Collections, and Programs; Peter Reed, Senior Deputy Director, Curatorial Affairs; Todd Bishop, Senior Deputy Director, External Affairs; and Patty Lipshutz, Secretary and General Counsel. We have also been fortunate to work with Diana Pulling (Office of the Director); Kim Mitchell, Margaret Doyle, Janelle Grace, Paul Jackson, and Meg Montgoris (Communications); Jessica Cash and John Champlin (Exhibition Planning & Administration); and Aaron Louis, Charlie Kalinowski, Tal Marks, Greg Singer, Steve Warrington, Edward D'Inzillo, and Michael Lefanto (Information Technology).

We acknowledge valuable advice and collegial encouragement from the current Chief Curators as well as from former Chief Curator of Photography Peter Galassi and former Chief Curator at Large Kynaston McShine. The project was also enriched by fruitful exchanges with colleagues in the Film Department: Sally Berger, Kitty Cleary, Sean Egan, Clay Farland, Andy Haas, Jytte Jensen, Mary Keene, Nancy Lukacinsky, Ron Magliozzi, Anne Morra, Justin Rigby, Josh Siegel, Charles Silver, Ashley Swinnerton, Katie Trainor, Pierre Vaz, Arthur Wehrhahn, John Weidner, and Peter Williamson. Finally, we applaud Laurence Kardish, former Senior Curator in the Department of Film, for his years of research into, writing on, and exhibition of German film at the museum, which played no small part in our own celebration of contemporary German filmmakers at MoMA.

We are most grateful to have collaborated with the Department of Publications, whose excellence, patience, and professionalism helped us create what we hope will be a seminal resource in contemporary film studies. We acknowledge Christopher Hudson, Publisher; Chul R. Kim, Associate Publisher; Marc Sapir, Production Director; Matthew Pimm, Production Manager; and Genevieve Allison, Image Rights Coordinator, for their valuable input throughout the entire process. David Frankel, Editorial Director, offered always thorough and thoughtful guidance; and our tireless book editor, Nancy Grubb, did a super job of shaping our thoughts and texts with precision and care. Translator Russell Stockman facilitated the exchange of ideas from Berlin to New York and helped parse subtle nuances where they mattered the most. The texts benefited from the efforts of peer reviewer Marco Abel, who shared his expertise on the topic and was helpful at every turn. Sincere thanks go to book designer Pascale Willi for the handsome design that skillfully embodies the essence of the moving images at hand.

This volume was enriched by Christoph Höchhausler, Dennis Lim, Katja Nicodemus, and Dr. Rainer Rother, who contributed intelligent and insightful texts in spite of tight deadlines that, ironically, collided with the Berlinale. We also offer many thanks to Christian Petzold and Nina Hoss for sharing their thoughts and insights in their interviews.

Above all, this project owes the most to the filmmakers: Maren Ade, Thomas Arslan, Valeska Grisebach, Benjamin Heisenberg, Christoph Hochhäusler, Ulrich Köhler, Pia Marais, Christian Petzold, Angela Schanelec, Maria Speth, Isabelle Stever, Nicolas Wackerbarth, and Henner Winckler. We thank them for opening up their work and process to us and also for the many crucial roles they played in the project—as artists, writers, producers, research contacts, and image sources. We are especially indebted to Christoph Hochhäusler, not only for his text but also for being a tremendous resource in his capacity as coeditor of *Revolver*. We extend thanks to Thomas Arslan, Valeska Grisebach, and Benjamin Heisenberg for joining their voices to the essays in the book with texts reprinted from *Revolver*. We intend this volume to be an artist's book as much as a scholar's or a film-lover's book, and we hope to have done justice to our generous and inspired interlocutors: the filmmakers themselves.

The Berlin International Film Festival, or Berlinale, has been a nurturing advocate for Berlin School filmmakers for nearly two decades. We thank our friends at the festival for their assistance in developing this exhibition, notably Dieter Kosslick, Wieland Speck, Christoph Terhechte, Thomas Hailer, Karin Hoffinger, and Linda Söffker.

The following image sources were both helpful and gracious in their permissions: Arne Höhne, Arne Höhne Press; Ina Plöttner, BRmedia; Viviana Kammel, Filmgalerie 451; Michael Kitzberger, Geyrhalter Film; Evelyn Holzendorf, Global Screen; Zsuzsanna Kiràly, Komplizen Film; Barbara Suhren and Christian Suhren, Peripher Filmverleih; Peter Heilrath, Peter Heilrath Film; Michael Weber and Florian Koerner von Gustorf, Schramm Film; Lisa Schrepf, teamWorx; Juergen Duerrwald, WDR; and Stefan Patzig, ZDF. Additionally, we thank the following photographers and cinematographers, whose images were the starting point for the publication's aesthetic: Hans Fromm, Christian Schulz, and Reinhold Vorschneider, as well as Florian Braun, Miguel Dieterich, Joachim Gern, Arlett Mattescheck, Hubert Mican, Patrick Orth, Stephan Rabold, Tom Trambow, Julia von Vietinghoff, Gudrun Widlok, and Michael Wiesweg. Special thanks to Komplizen Film and Maren Ade for the seductive cover image.

We are particularly pleased to enrich this exhibition with public programming organized in conjunction with Deutsches Haus at New York University; many thanks to Martin Rauchbauer and Juliane Camfield, our partners in that endeavor. We also acknowledge the Goethe-Institut New York and German Films for their support of German cultural projects in New York.

For helping us take this project from the page to the screen, we express our gratitude to the producers and distributors who have made possible the exhibition of the films themselves, which is the first extensive survey of Berlin School films in New York. We thank the producers Bettina Brokemper, Heimatfilm; Katrin Schlösser, ö Filmproduktion; Christoph Friedel and Claudia Steffen, Pandora; Peter Stockhaus, Peter Stockhaus Filmproduktion; and Michael Weber and Florian Koerner von Gustorf, Schramm Film. We furthermore extend our appreciation to the distributors Jeff Lipsky, Adopt Films; Anke Hahn, Deutsche Kinemathek; Jean-Christophe Simon, Films Boutique; Marine Rechard, Films Distribution; Gisela Wiltschik and Claudia Rudolph, Global Screen; Sebastian Püttner, Heimatfilm; Joe Dreier, Hollywood Classics; Michael Weber, The Match Factory; Peter Rommel, Peter Rommel Filmproduktion; Peter Stockhaus, Peter Stockhaus Filmproduktion; and Solveig Langeland, Sola-Media.

We wish to offer our personal thanks to Karen Arikian, Alan Goodwin, Wilma Harzenetter, Alfred Holighaus, Binali Karatas, James Latimer, Johanna Muth, Katja Nicodemus, Marc Ohrem-Leclef, Christiane Peitz, Peter Polzer, Ruth Roy, and Verena von Stackelberg.

Finally, we want to acknowledge the critical contributions of Sophie Cavoulacos, Curatorial Assistant in the Department of Film. She demonstrated an ability to work quickly, graciously, and meticulously across oceans and language barriers. It is because of her dedication that we were able to focus primarily on the content rather than the construction of this book, and for that we will be forever grateful.

Rajendra Roy
The Celeste Bartos Chief Curator of Film

Anke Leweke

Suggestions for Further Reading

BOOKS, CATALOGUES, AND DISSERTATIONS

Abel, Marco. *The Counter-Cinema of the Berlin School.* Rochester, N.Y.: Camden House, forthcoming.

Borges, Christian, and Martine Floch, eds. *Novo Cinema independente alemão: Uma Outra Politica do olhar.* São Paulo: Centro Cultural Banco do Brasil, 2009.

Cook, Roger F., Lutz Koepnick, Kristin Kopp, and Brad Prager, eds. *Berlin School Glossary: An ABC of the New Wave in German Cinema.* Bristol, England: Intellect, 2013.

Cooke, Paul. *Contemporary German Cinema.* Manchester, England: Manchester University Press, 2012.

Fisher, Jaimey. *Christian Petzold.* Urbana: University of Illinois Press, forthcoming.

Gras, Pierre. *Goodbye Fassbinder! Le Cinéma allemand depuis la réunification.* Paris: Éditions Jacqueline Chambon, 2011.

Heberlein, Jana. *Die neue Berliner Schule: Zwischen Verflachung und Tiefe: Ein ästhetisches Spannungsfeld in den Filmen von Angela Schanelec.* Stuttgart: Ibidem-Verl., 2012.

Jamal, Aisha. "Investigating Contemporary German National Identity, Ethnicity and Belonging in Films and Filmmakers of Immigrant Descent." Ph.D. diss., University of Toronto, 2009.

Neubauer, Jochen. *Türkische Deutsche, Kanakster und Deutschländer: Identität und Fremdwahrnehmung in Film und Literatur: Fatih Akin, Thomas Arslan, Emine Sevgi Özdamar, Zafer Şenocak und Feridun Zaimoglu.* Würzburg: Königshausen & Neumann, 2011.

Rother, Rainer. *Nina Hoss: "Ich muss mir jeden Satz glauben": Ein Porträt.* Leipzig: Henschel, 2009.

Schwenk, Johanna. *Leerstellen—Resonanzräume: Zur Ästhetik der Auslassung im Werk des Filmregisseurs Christian Petzold.* Baden-Baden: Nomos, 2012.

ARTICLES AND ESSAYS

Abel, Marco. "Tender Speaking: An Interview with Christoph Hochhäusler." *Senses of Cinema* 42 (January–March 2007), http://sensesofcinema.com/2007/42/christoph-hochhausler/.

——. "'The Cinema of Identification Gets on My Nerves': An Interview with Christian Petzold." *Cineaste* 33, no. 3 (Summer 2008), http://www.cineaste.com/articles/an-interview-with-christian-petzold.htm.

——. "Intensifying Life: The Cinema of the 'Berlin School.'" *Cineaste* 33, no. 4 (Fall 2008), http://www.cineaste.com/articles/the-berlin-school.htm.

——. "Imaging Germany: The (Political) Cinema of Christian Petzold." In *The Collapse of the Conventional: German Film and Its Politics at the Turn of the Twenty-first Century,* edited by Jaimey Fisher and Brad Prager, pp. 258–84. Detroit: Wayne State University Press, 2010.

——. "'A Sharpening of Our Regard': Realism, Affect and the Redistribution of the Sensible in Valeska Grisebach's *Longing.*" In *New Directions in German Cinema,* edited by Paul Cooke and Chris Homewood, pp. 204–22. London and New York: I. B. Tauris, 2011.

——. "The Minor Cinema of Thomas Arslan: A Prolegomenon." In *Turkish German Cinema in the New Millennium: Sites, Sounds, and Screens,* edited by Sabine Hake and Barbara Caroline Mennel, pp. 44–55. New York: Berghahn Books, 2012.

——. "22 January 2007: The Establishment Strikes Back: The Counter-Cinema of the 'Berlin School' and Its Rejection by the German Film Industry Establishment." In *A New History of German Cinema,* edited by Jennifer M. Kapczynski and Michael D. Richardson, pp. 602–8. Rochester, N.Y.: Camden House, 2012.

Arslan, Thomas. "Kinoerfahrungen." *Revolver* 13 (December 2005): 92–101.

Baron, Esther. "Zukunft Kino." *Kinema Kommunal,* no. 1 (January/February/March 2008): 2–3.

Baute, Michael, Ekkehard Knörer, Volker Pantenburg, Stefan Pethke, and Simon Rothöhler. "'Berliner Schule'—Eine Collage." *Kolik.film* 6 (October 2006): 7–14. Published in English as "The Berlin School: A Collage," *Senses of Cinema*, no. 55 (July 2010), http://sensesofcinema.com/2010/feature-articles/the-berlin-school---a-collage-2/.

Benoliel, Bernard. "*Bungalow* d'Ulrich Köhler: Identification d'un personnage." *Cinéma—Revue semestrielle d'esthéthique et d'histoire du cinéma* 6 (Autumn 2003): 70–78.

Chauvin, Jean-Sébastien. "Jeunes auteurs en force." *Cahiers du cinéma* 575 (January 2003): 28–29.

———. "Allemagne: Génération esseulée." *Cahiers du cinéma* 652 (January 2010): 52.

Delorme, Stéphane. "Passager, clandestin." *Cahiers du cinéma* 617 (November 2006): 17–18.

Eisenreich, Pierre. "Christian Petzold: Se situer entre deux mondes, le passé et le present." *Positif* 615 (May 2012): 21–25.

Finzi, Pierre-Emmanuel. "Voyage d'École: Le Cinéma berlinois." *Art Press*, special issue (August/September/October 2006): 83–90.

Fisher, Jaimey. "German *Autoren* Dialogue with Hollywood? Refunctioning the Horror Genre in Christian Petzold's *Yella*." In *New Directions in German Cinema*, edited by Paul Cooke and Chris Homewood, pp. 223–38. London and New York: I. B. Tauris, 2011.

Ganz, Antonia. "Interview: Angela Schanelec." *Revolver* 5 (September 2001): 98–105.

Graf, Dominik, Christian Petzold, and Christoph Hochhäusler. "Mailwechsel Berliner Schule." *Revolver* 16 (May 2007): 6–41. Excerpts published in English as *Dreileben*, http://www.berlinale.de/external/de/filmarchiv/doku_pdf/20113081.pdf.

Gras, Pierre. "Qui regarde l'Allemagne? À propos des films de Christian Petzold et d'Angela Schanelec." *Cinéma—Revue semestrielle d'esthéthique et d'histoire du cinéma* 9 (Spring 2005): 106–15.

Grisebach, Valeska. "Von hier aus." *Revolver* 16 (May 2007): 74–93.

Hasted, Nick. "In the Shadow of the Wall." *Sight & Sound* 22, no. 10 (October 2012): 48–51.

Heisenberg, Benjamin. "Form Follows." *Revolver* 3 (June 1999): 102–7.

———. "Narration." *Revolver* 12 (May 2005): 84–93.

Herrmann, Ulrich. "Figur fürs Leben: Gespräch mit Maren Ade." In *Stoff: Von der Idee zum Drehbuch*, pp. 43–53. Frankfurt: Verlag der Autoren, 2005.

Hochhäusler, Christoph. "Kino der Herausforderung." *Revolver* 11 (September 2004): 28–37. Published in English as "A Cinema of Challenge," *Vertigo* (England) 3, no. 5 (Spring 2007): 6.

Hochhäusler, Christoph, and Nicolas Wackerbarth. "Gespräch 'Neue Realistische Schule?' mit Maren Ade, Sylke Enders, Sören Voigt, Henner Winckler." *Revolver* 11 (September 2004): 72–119.

———. "Interview: Angela Schanelec, Reinhold Vorschneider." *Revolver* 13 (December 2005): 6–43.

———. "Interview: Ulrich Köhler, Patrick Orth." *Revolver* 16 (May 2007): 43–70.

———. "Interview: Tankred Dorst + Ursula Ehler." *Revolver* 18 (January 2008): 60–87.

Kirsten, Guido. "Fiktionale Authenzität und die Unterklausel im Zuschauervertrag: Zum filmischen Realismus in Henner Wincklers *Klassenfahrt*." In *Kino in Bewegung: Perspektiven des deutschen Gegenwartsfilms*, edited by Thomas Schick and Tobias Ebbrecht, pp. 105–20. Wiesbaden: VS Verlag für Sozialwissenschaften, 2011.

Knörer, Ekkehard. "Luminous Days: Notes on the New German Cinema." *Vertigo* (England) 3, no. 5 (Spring 2007): 3–5.

Köhler, Ulrich. "Warum ich keine 'politischen' Filme mache." *New Filmkritik*, April 23, 2007, http://newfilmkritik.de/archiv/2007-04/warum-ich-keine-politischen-filme-mache. Published in English as "Why I Don't Make 'Political' Films," *Cinema Scope* 38 (2009): 10–13.

———. "Warum nicht einfach die Wahrheit?" *Revolver* 18 (June 2008): 23–38.

Kopp, Kristin. "Christoph Hochhäusler's *This Very Moment*: The Berlin School and the Politics of Spatial Aesthetics in the German-Polish Borderlands." In *The Collapse of the Conventional: German Film and Its Politics at the Turn of the Twenty-first Century*, edited by Jaimey Fisher and Brad Prager, pp. 285–308. Detroit: Wayne State University Press, 2010.

Lehnguth, Henrike. "Sleepers, Informants, and the Everyday: Theorizing Terror and Ambiguity in Benjamin Heisenberg's *Schläfer*." In *From Solidarity to Schisms: 9/11 and After in Fiction and Film from Outside the U.S.*, edited by Cara Cilano, pp. 115–30. Amsterdam and New York: Rodopi, 2009.

Lequeret, Elisabeth. "Allemagne: La Génération de l'espace." *Cahiers du cinéma* 587 (February 2004): 47–51.

———. "Vague allemande." *Cahiers du cinéma* 598 (February 2005): 20–22.

———. "Printemps allemand." *Cahiers du cinéma* 609 (February 2006): 45–48.

———. "Angela Schanelec, un après-midi avec elle." *Cahiers du cinéma* 622 (April 2007): 64.

Leweke, Anke. "Der neue deutsche Film ist da!" *Tip Berlin*, no. 22 (1998): 19.

———. "Ausgesetzt." *Die Zeit*, November 11, 2004, p. 51.

———. "Berliner Phantome." *Die Zeit*, September 15, 2005, p. 53. Published in English as "Berlin's Ghosts," http://www.signandsight.com/features/375.html.

———. "Der Rhythmus des Lebens." *Die Tageszeitung*, January 9, 2007, Kultur, p. 21.

———. "Das Kino der schönen Wege." *Die Zeit*, July 7, 2011, p. 53.

Lim, Dennis. "A German Wave, Focused on Today." *New York Times*, May 10, 2009, Arts and Leisure, p. 16.

———. "Worlds of Possibilities: Christian Petzold, Dominik Graf, and Christoph Hochhäusler's *Dreileben*." *Cinema Scope* 46 (Spring 2011): 40–41.

———. "Summoning Halcyon Days of Failed Ideals: Christian Petzold Directs 'Barbara,' Starring Nina Hoss." *New York Times*, December 9, 2012, Arts and Leisure, p. 17.

Löffler, Petra. "Ghost Sounds und die kinematographische Imagination: Christian Petzolds *Gespenster* und *Yella*." In *Kino in Bewegung: Perspektiven des deutschen Gegenwartsfilms*, edited by Thomas Schick and Tobias Ebbrecht, pp. 63–78. Wiesbaden: VS Verlag für Sozialwissenschaften, 2011.

Méranger, Thierry. "Trois rencontres allemandes: Christoph Hochhäusler." *Cahiers du cinéma* 662 (December 2010): 31–32.

Möller, Olaf. "Das Mögliche machen, so Weiteres möglich machen." *New Filmkritik*, July 7, 2007, http://newfilmkritik.de/archiv/2007-07/das-mogliche-machen-so-weiteres-moglich-machen/.

———. "Vanishing Point." *Sight & Sound* 17, no. 10 (October 2007): 40–42.

Nicodemus, Katja. "Cruising Kreuzberg." *Tip Berlin*, no. 25 (1997): 42.

———. "Distanz und Freiheit." *Die Tageszeitung*, February 10, 2001, Kultur, p. 26.

———. "Die ersten Mohikaner—Die Berliner Firma Schramm-Film macht das beste deutsche Kino." *Die Zeit*, April 25, 2002, p. 43.

Nicodemus, Katja, and Christof Siemes. "'Arm filmt gut? Das gefällt mir nicht.'" *Die Zeit*, January 9, 2009, p. 41.

Nord, Cristina. "Notizen zur Berliner Schule." *New Filmkritik*, July 7, 2007, http://newfilmkritik.de/archiv/2007-07/notizen-zur-berliner-schule/.

Peitz, Christiane. "Die Taktgeberin." *Der Tagesspiegel*, March 6, 2012, Kultur, p. 21.

Peranson, Mark. "Me, You, & Everyone They Know: A Conversation with Maren Ade." *Cinema Scope* 40 (Fall 2009): 6–11.

———. "Not Political Cinema: Ulrich Köhler's *Sleeping Sickness*." *Cinema Scope* 46 (Spring 2011): 37–39.

Petzold, Christian. "H0." *Revolver* 5 (September 2001): 64–71.

Polak-Springer, Katrin. "On the Difficulties of Letting the Other Speak: The German-Polish Relationship in Christoph Hochhäusler's 'Milchwald.'" *Edge—A Graduate Journal for German and Scandinavian Studies* 2 (2011), no. 1, http://scholarworks.umass.edu/edge/vol2/iss1/2/.

Rebhandl, Bert. "Prinzipielle Gesetzlosigkeit: Neuere deutsche Genrefilme reflektieren die Grundlagen des Erzählens." In *Die Lust am Genre: Verbrechergeschichten aus Deutschland*, edited by Rainer Rother and Julia Pattis, pp. 159–68. Berlin: Bertz + Fischer, 2011.

Rentschler, Eric. "Declaration of Independents: Eric Rentschler on the 50th Anniversary of the Oberhausen Manifesto." *Artforum* 50, no. 10 (Summer 2012): 272–79.

———. "School's Out." *Artforum* 51, no. 9 (May 2013): 99–100, 102.

Schanelec, Angela. "Marseille 1.–10. März." *New Filmkritik*, March 12, 2002, http://newfilmkritik.de/archiv/2002-03/marseille-1-10-marz/.

———. "Das Licht selbst filmen." *Die Tageszeitung*, March 14, 2013, Kultur, p. 15.

Seesslen, Georg. "Die Anti-Erzählmaschine." *Freitag*, September 14, 2007, http://www.freitag.de/autoren/der-freitag/die-anti-erzahlmaschine.

Sicinski, Michael. "Once the Wall Has Tumbled: Christian Petzold's *Jerichow*." *Cinema Scope* 38 (Spring 2009): 6–9.

———. "Making Of." *Cargo* 7 (September 16, 2010): 22–35.

Stevens, Isabel. "Three Lives." *Sight & Sound* 21, no. 11 (November 2011): 30.

Tracy, Andrew. "States of Longing: Films from the Berlin School." *Notebook*, March 2, 2009, http://mubi.com/notebook/posts/states-of-longing-films-from-the-berlin-school.

von Lucke, Philipp. "Interview: Reinhold Vorschneider." *Film & TV Kameramann* 3 (2011): 6–12.

Wackerbarth, Nicolas. "Tableau Vivant." *Revolver* 13 (December 2005): 126–33.

Wagner, Brigitta B. "Vorschneider in Focus." *Film Quarterly* 63, no. 4 (Summer 2010): 62–64.

Wheatley, Catherine. "Fire Eats the Soul." *Sight & Sound* 17, no. 6 (June 2007): 44–45.

———. "Not Politics but People: The 'Feminine Aesthetic' of Valeska Grisebach and Jessica Hausner." In *New Austrian Film*, edited by Robert Dassanowsky and Oliver C. Speck, pp. 136–47. New York: Berghahn Books, 2011.

Wolf, Sabine. "Die urbane Landschaft in den Filmen der Berliner Schule." *Cinema* 54 (2009): 39–50.

Zwiebel, Ralf. "Reparation and the Empathetic Other: Christian Petzold's *Wolfsburg*." In *Projected Shadows: Psychoanalytic Reflections on the Representation of Loss in European Cinema*, edited by Andrea Sabbadini, pp. 56–64. Hove, England, and New York: Routledge, 2007.

Index of Names and Titles

Page numbers in *italics* refer to illustrations.

Credits

In reproducing the images contained in this publication, the Museum obtained the permission of the rights holders whenever possible. In those instances where the Museum could not locate the rights holders, notwithstanding good-faith efforts, it requests that any contact information concerning such rights holders be forwarded so that they may be contacted for future editions.

Maren Ade. *Alle Anderen*
Film stills. © Florian Braun/Komplizen Film.
Courtesy Komplizen Film
Cover and pp. 56, 86–87

Maren Ade. *Der Wald vor lauter Bäumen*
Film still. © and courtesy Komplizen Film
P. 49

Thomas Arslan. *Dealer*
Film still. Michael Wiesweg. © Trans-Film.
Courtesy Peripher Filmverleih
P. 78

Thomas Arslan. *Der schöne Tag*
Film stills. © and courtesy Filmgalerie 451
Pp. 24, 79
Production stills. © Christian Schulz.
Courtesy the filmmaker
Pp. 13, 79
Poster. © atelier doppelpunkt. Courtesy
Peripher Filmverleih
P. 22

Thomas Arslan. *Ferien*
Film still. Michael Wiesweg. © Pickpocket
Filmproduktion. Courtesy Peripher Filmverleih
P. 81

Thomas Arslan. *Geschwister*
Film still. © and courtesy Filmgalerie 451
P. 78
Production stills. © Christian Schulz.
Courtesy the filmmaker
Pp. 74, 82–83

Thomas Arslan. *Gold*
Film stills. Patrick Orth. © Schramm Film.
Courtesy Arne Höhne Press
Pp. 61, 64, 65, 72–73, 75, 76

Thomas Arslan. *Im Schatten*
Film stills. Reinhold Vorschneider. © Schramm Film.
Courtesy Peripher Filmverleih
P. 77

Thomas Arslan. *Mach die Musik leiser*
Film still. © Thomas Arslan/Schramm Film.
Courtesy the filmmaker
P. 14

Dominik Graf. *Komm mir nicht nach*, from *Dreileben*
Film still. © ARD/ Degeto Film/Julia von Vietinghoff.
Courtesy WDR
P. 95

Valeska Grisebach. *Sehnsucht*
Film stills. © Peter Rommel Filmproduktion.
Courtesy Arne Höhne Press
Pp. 66–67, 92

Benjamin Heisenberg. *Die Räuber*
Production stills. © Hubert Mican. Courtesy
Geyrhalter Film/Peter Heilrath Film
Pp. 88, 89
Production stills. © Miguel Dieterich. Courtesy
Geyrhalter Film/Peter Heilrath Film
Pp. 94, 97

Benjamin Heisenberg
Photographs. © Benjamin Heisenberg
Pp. 98–101

Christoph Hochhäusler. *Eine Minute Dunkel*,
from *Dreileben*
Film still. © Heimatfilm/WDR/Reinhold Vorschneider.
Courtesy Global Screen
P. 95

Christoph Hochhäusler. *Falscher Bekenner*
Film stills. © Heimatfilm. Courtesy Arne Höhne Press
Pp. 20, 24, 26

Christoph Hochhäusler. *Milchwald*
Film stills. © and courtesy Filmgalerie 451
Pp. 27, 29, 91

Christoph Hochhäusler. *Unter dir die Stadt*
Film stills. © Heimatfilm. Courtesy Arne Höhne Press
Pp. 18–19, 94
Production stills. © Tom Trambow. Courtesy
the filmmaker
P. 21

Ulrich Köhler. *Bungalow*
Film stills. © and courtesy Filmgalerie 451
Pp. 23, 26

Ulrich Köhler. *Montag kommen die Fenster*
Film stills. © and courtesy Filmgalerie 451
Pp. 27, 44–45, 55

Christian Petzold. *Barbara*
Film still. © Schramm Film/Hans Fromm
Pp. 30–31
Production stills. Christian Schulz. © Schramm Film.
Courtesy Schramm Film
Pp. 13, 32, 33, 34, 58–59, 63

Christian Petzold. *Die Beischlafdiebin*
Film still. © ZDF/Gudrun Widlok. Courtesy ZDF
P. 17

Christian Petzold. *Die innere Sicherheit*
Film stills. © Schramm Film/Hans Fromm
Pp. 39, 41, 50